Middlesex Vol II
Edited by Sarah Marshall

Young Writers
First published in Great Britain in 2004 by:
Young Writers
Remus House
Coltsfoot Drive
Peterborough
PE2 9JX
Telephone: 01733 890066
Website: www.youngwriters.co.uk

All Rights Reserved

© *Copyright Contributors 2004*

SB ISBN 1 84460 452 7

Foreword

Young Writers was established in 1991 and has been passionately devoted to the promotion of reading and writing in children and young adults ever since. The quest continues today. Young Writers remains as committed to engendering the fostering of burgeoning poetic and literary talent as ever.

This year's Young Writers competition has proven as vibrant and dynamic as ever and we are delighted to present a showcase of the best poetry from across the UK. Each poem has been carefully selected from a wealth of *Once Upon A Rhyme* entries before ultimately being published in this, our twelfth primary school poetry series.

Once again, we have been supremely impressed by the overall high quality of the entries we have received. The imagination, energy and creativity which has gone into each young writer's entry made choosing the best poems a challenging and often difficult but ultimately hugely rewarding task - the general high standard of the work submitted amply vindicating this opportunity to bring their poetry to a larger appreciative audience.

We sincerely hope you are pleased with our final selection and that you will enjoy *Once Upon A Rhyme Middlesex Vol II* for many years to come.

Contents

Amir Amraie (10)   1

Alexandra Junior School
Haaniah Hamid (9)	1
Gurinder Rayat (9)	2
Manraj Ubhi (8)	2
Hema Gautam (9)	3
Yasmin Khatri (9)	3
Harpreet Phull (8)	3
Sian Bhatti (9) & Caitlin Seaman	4
Sehar Mir (8)	4
Wiktoria Wiszenko (9)	4
Priyanka Jethwa (8)	5
Rima Shah (8)	5
Srishti Neogi (9)	6
Yasmine Mansouri	6
Priya Gupta (9)	7
Sian Bhatti (9)	7
Ifia Chaudhri	8
Wajidur Rahman	8
Christine	9
Kaiya Adams	9
Khezer Ismail	9
Harvir Ubhi	10
Shahzain Syed	10
Balpreet	11
Matteo	11
Aleesha Toor (9)	12
Freddy Farias (9)	12
Mateusz Kryba	13
Roda Hassan (9)	13
Yasmin Chahal (9)	14
Alfaz Brepotra (9)	14
Sidorela Gjeci (9)	15
Nikita Mehtaj	15
Jasdeep Kaur Bansal (8)	16
Gin	16
Jae Letch (9)	16
Sarandeep Kaur Judge (9)	17

Zeeshan Deen (8)	17
Frankie Romp	17
Premal Shah	18
Luca	18
Dylan Angelidakis	18
Shuhada Khanom (8)	19

Andrew Ewing Primary School

Indpal Kaur Kullar (10)	19
Ricky Garcha (10)	20
Jasmine Kaur Pank (11)	21
Shivam Bansal (11)	22
Gautam Tankaria (10)	22
Bavneet Kaur Aulakh (11)	23
Simran Kaur Kahlon	23
Charlotte Richardson (10)	24
Pavandeep Kaur (11)	24
Bushra Nasim (10)	25
Tomas James Dyerson (11)	26
Taylor Rowlands (10)	27

Archdeacon Cambridge's CE Primary School

Jacob Hamblin-Pyke (9)	27
Cecilia Rose McCormick (8)	28
Alice Coaker Basdell (9)	28
Sam Foley (8)	28
Craig Henry (8)	29
Jenanne Soboh (8)	29
Peter Gorbutt (9)	29
Elliott Morley (8)	30
Jeremy Laing (8)	30
Elliot Tomos Webb (8)	30
Molly Purdue-Guy (8)	31
Jessica Pead (8)	31
Oliver Foudah (9)	32
Meg Riley (8)	32
John Stanley (8)	33
Emilia Marshall (8)	33
Charlotte Kelsted (9)	33
Stephanie Knight (9)	34
Michael Oliver Capon (9)	34

Albert Ewin (9)   34
Ria St Hilaire (9)   35
Clarissa Jeffery (9)   35
Louise Breckon (9)   35
Matthew Harris (9)   36
Raad Begh (8)   36

Ashton House School
Dariush Salek (8)   36
Radheka Agarwal (9)   37
Harry Bourne (9)   37
Natalie Watts (10)   38
Emily Ann Watson (10)   38
Iman Jasani (9)   39
Aaron Singh Saran (8)   39
Waseem Sayid (11)   40
Josh Thakrar (8)   40
Umair Mughal (11)   41
Jaipal Sachdev (10)   41
Ruchit Gupta Chaudhary (11)   42
Priya Grewal (11)   43
Zaqi Ismail (11)   44
Khimi Grewal (11)   44
Amanjai Sharma (11)   45
MinWoo Park (9)   46
Nishita Agarwal (9)   46
Anique Joubert (9)   47
Hassan Qureshi (8)   48

Aylward First & Middle School
Amal Ismail (12)   48
Savannah Greenaway Bailey (11)   49
Ellen O'Brien (12)   49
Gemma Kilkenny (12)   49
Bobby Bloch (10)   50
Hailey Parker (12)   50
Hayley Wright (11)   51
Jessica Puplett (12)   51
Natasha Jayne Britton (12)   51
Ahmed Adelabu (12)   52
Elizabeth Rose Bogue (11)   52

Amélia Sheikh (11)	53
Dettori Shek (11)	53
Victoria Lewis (12)	54
Tahlia Theresa Lewington (11)	54
Ayan Yussuf (11)	54
Zainab Reza (11)	55
Rebecca Louise Varley (11)	55
Nekhel Ramavrat (11)	56
Holly Jobling (12)	56
Chanelle Ellington (8)	57
Sean Young (11)	57
Lincoln Leech (7)	58
Jamie Edwards (11)	58
Sheiyaan Ahmed (8)	59
Anam Soroya (12)	59
Lesley Warrington (7)	60
Dawn Pearson (11)	60
Gavin Law (7)	61
Jonathon Lewington (8)	61
Dora Leaman (8)	62
Michaela O'Brien (11)	62
Riddhi Thakrar (7)	63
Mohamed Mohamed (8)	63
Disha Patel (8)	64
Sam Marks (7)	64
Zulfikar Zaffar (8)	64
Jordan Turner (7)	65
Kirsty Lewington (9)	65
Hamzah Ahmed (8)	66
Jenisha Patel (8)	66
Adam James (7)	67
Terrell Richards-Gayle (8)	67
Sophie Tan (8)	67
Donna Edwards (8)	68
Saada Shuwa (8)	68
Danielle Swift (8)	68
Dean Davey (8)	69
Lewis Gray (7)	69
Francesca Pagliaroli (7)	69
Mohammed Dedhar (8)	70
Kevin Da Mata (8)	70
Fiona Berbatovci (8)	70

Bishop Perrin School
Abigail Ross (10)	71
Sophie Hopkins	71
Robert Kirkham (10)	72
Lydia Clarke (11)	72
Chloe Penson (11)	73
Emily Dumbrell (11)	73
Joshua Dowden (11)	74
Katie-Marie Waygood (10)	74
Rebekah Wiltshire (10)	74
Charlotte Cleveland (11)	75
Hannah Thornley	75
Jacob Modak (10)	76
Rhys Wilson (10)	76
Catherine Hale (11)	77
Jack Collis	77
Ben Crane (10)	78
Adam G Bull (10)	78
Grace McKeown (10)	79
Vanessa Hill	79
Manoj Athukorala (11)	80
Rahil Davda (11)	80

Crane Park Primary School
Brandon Robinson (11)	80
Harjit Padda (11)	81
Jasvinder Singh (10)	81
Michael Paul Rosato (10)	82
Josh Kearney (10)	82
Brendan Stanbridge (11)	82
Ashley Martins (10)	83
Michael Pereira (10)	83
Rochelle Green (10)	84
Jade Hammett (10)	84
Samantha Bragg (11)	85
Eric Osei Tutu (10)	85
Georgia-May Cooper (11)	86
Kiana Jade Rhianna Smith (10)	86
Ella May Gibson (10)	87
Shivani Patel (11)	87
Shahnaz Islam (11)	88

Nilofar Afzali (10)	88
Yousof Yosofzai (10)	89
Hamed Alemzada (10)	89
Chanel Downes (11)	90
Jade Rayner-Jones (10)	90
Chloe Shaw (10)	91
Callum Creighton (10)	91
Emma O'Brien (10)	92
Kiran Singh (10)	92
Kuljit Padda (11)	93

Dormers Wells Junior School

Aasia Najumi (7)	93
Simran Juttla (8)	93
Shaun Rockall (8)	94
Ikram Musse (7)	94
Vickram Singh (8)	94
Ali Abbas (7)	94
Shiala Suleman (8)	95
Dwayne Boyce (8)	95
Amardeep Dosanjh (8)	96
Akash Gurung (10)	96
Humaira Aslam (9)	97
Abdurahman Mohammed (8)	97
Anesu Madamombe (9)	98
Mohamed Omar (9)	98
Steven Gangadeen (8)	99
Sara Haider (9)	99
Maham Qureshi (9)	100
Femisha Patel (8)	100
Saminder Brar & Sanjay Mall (10)	101
Shanka Fernando & Daman Johal (11)	101

Echelford Primary School

Sophie Pearson (10)	101
Sheena Petrovini (11)	102
Russell Ashwood (11)	102
David Merchant (11)	103
Leah Bulley (11)	103
Adam Huse (11)	104
Andrew Salt (11)	104

Jamie Cork (10)	105
Lora Thomas (11)	105
Kelly Woods (11)	106
Hannah Wakeman (11)	106
Georgia Grant (10)	107
Chelby Meade (10)	107
Georgia Page (10)	108
Tom Dunbar (8)	108
Fay Yeoman (11)	108
Greg Giles (11)	109
Michael Adamson (10)	109
David Gudge (10)	109
Stuart Donald (10)	110
Jack Cooper (8)	110
Zoe Stanton (10)	110
Lucy Thurlow (10)	111
Christina Cope (11)	111
Maria Stanton (10)	112
Sian Louise Thomas (10)	112
Ben Skilling (10)	112
Chloe Clark (10)	113
Liam O'Shea (11)	113
Shyam Petrovini (11)	114
Andrew Trott (11)	114
Bridie Smithers (9)	115
Jessie Beetham (11)	115
Lauren Meadows (9)	116
Glenn Olding (11)	116
Luke Rogers (9)	117
Samantha Bromley (9)	118
Samuel Tucker (10) & Ben Paget (11)	118
Melissa Soden (9)	119
David Amaddio (11)	119
Joseph Swabey (9)	120
Josh Guidera (10)	121
Hannah McDonough (10)	122
Charles Whitley (9)	122
Emma Burrows (9)	123
Joe Taberer (11)	123
Chloe Boon (10)	124
Tom McNab (10)	124
Molly Nash (9)	125

Shayla Ash (10)	125
Matthew Rogers (11)	126
Ross Grant (9)	126
Harry Jackman (10)	126
Ellouise Holley (10)	127
Tasmin Arnould (9)	127
Nathan Keeley (8)	128
Jodie Knowles (10)	128
Zoe High (9)	128
Bill Clack (9)	129
Elliot Bernath (9)	129
Connor Christmas (9)	130
Shenice Baptiste (9)	130
Carrie Lee Holman (10)	131
Michael Arbon (9)	131
Tyler Fraser-Coombe (10)	132
Katie Simms (9)	132
Jack Dunbar (8)	133

Edgware Junior School

Isaac Lyndsay (11)	133
Priscilla Osoba (10)	134
Alexander Zendra (8)	134
Samantha Sivapragasam (9)	135
Runako Munyoro (8)	135
Rosie Watts (9)	136
Faisal Iqbal (9)	136
Sara Failey (10)	137
Ronnie Creed (8)	137
Kundai Rusike (8)	138
Maariya Parkar (9)	138
Salva Ravan (10)	139
Halima Djeraoui (8)	140
Jade Lafferty (9)	140
Flynt Nicoll-Coker (8)	141
Eniola Dare (9)	141
Lubna Mahirban (11)	142
Josh McCormick (10)	142
Rhys Ellis (7)	143
Amber Sedki-Farag (7)	143

Highfield Primary School
   Grace Harrison (11)   144

Holland House School
   Rahul Thakrar (11)   145
   Phyllis Sowah (10)   145
   Gopi Sivakumaran (11)   146
   Shenal Shah (11)   147
   Caitlin Pinner (10)   148
   Sarah Chaplin (11)   148
   Alexander Lewis (10)   149
   Naikee Kohli (10)   150
   Kate Freedman (10)   151
   Elio Elia (10)   152
   Georgia Sears (10)   153

Longmead Primary School
   Joshua Alfred Gibbons (10)   153
   Luul Hussein (11)   154
   Sorath Soomro (10)   154
   Frankie Denslow (11)   155
   Elliott Barker (9)   155
   Uma Begum (9)   156
   Kayleigh Brown (10)   156
   Amy Kelvey (10)   156
   Amelio Ramkalawan (11)   157
   Emma Ashford (10)   157
   Hollie Ryder (10)   158
   Hannah Gardner (9)   158
   Zara Thorn (9)   159

Reddiford School
   Ambika Natesan (10)   159
   Shobana Sivalingam (10)   160
   Mustafaen Kamal (9)   161
   Priya Patel (10)   161
   Conor O'Brien (10)   162
   Shruti Dorai (9)   162
   Lawrence Xu (10)   163
   Niral Bharat (10)   164

Rishi Peshavaria (10)	164
Rishil Bhikha (9)	165
Robbie Singh (10)	165
Rikhil Shah (9)	166
Rupen Patel (9)	167
Niththilan Sritharan (8)	168
Ankit Patel (10)	168
Shivana Sood (10)	169
Jamie Tanna (9)	170
Misha Mansigani (11)	171
Haran Devakumar (10)	172
Amber-Rose Blogg (8)	172
Dominic Dichen (11)	173
Kishan Patel (10)	174
Meera Relwani (10)	175
Akash Alexander (11)	175
Zehra Saifuddin (11)	176
Olajide Olatunji (11)	177
Harin Bharadia (10)	177
Nicola Gartenberg (11)	178
Akshay Baldota (10)	178
Katie Walsh (11)	179
Nisha Patel (10)	180
Shil Shah (11)	180
Priyen Patel (10)	181
Feyi Onamusi (10)	181
Shamir Vekaria (10)	182
Shiv Mistry (11)	182
Helen Farmer (11)	183
Janaki Kava (10)	184
Neha Shukla (10)	185
Darshali Shah (9)	185
Anoli Mehta (10)	186
Jemie Irukwu (9)	186
Nirali Shah (8)	187
Karan Sihra (8)	187
Sonal D Patel (8)	188
Elisha Patel (9)	189
Sharukh Zuberi (8)	190
Nikita Radia (8)	190
Devika Chudasama (9)	191
Jonathan Collier (8)	192

Matthew Rodin (8)	193
Shivan P Lakhani (8)	193
Gabriel Rajan (9)	194
Kaveer Patel (8)	194
Tejuswi Patel (11)	195
William Kanagaratnam (8)	195
Kushal N Patel (9)	196
Kishan Ragunathan (l0)	197

St Stephen's CE Junior School, Twickenham

Freddie MacCormack (10)	197
Oscar Allan (9)	198
Edward McDonald (10)	199
Phoebe Evans (10)	200
Ben Bradshaw (8)	200
Eddy Reichwald (9)	201
Olivia Day (9)	202
Michael Howe (9)	203
Fionn McKnight (10)	203
Nathan King (9)	204
Louise Taylor (9)	205
Thomas Alington (10)	206
Max Ambler (9)	206
Christy Born (10)	207
Alice Hollyer (10)	207
Anna Smethurst (10)	208
Laura Goldup (9)	209
Eloise Cottey (9)	209
Sophie Collin (9)	210
Jack Gregory (10)	211
Mollie Borges (9)	212
Eve Carpenter (10)	213
Matthew Morris (9)	214
Maeve Gumbley (10)	214
Scarlett Rose Young (9)	215
Selena Bowdidge (10)	216
Faye Driver (8)	216
Abi Muir (11)	217
William Atkins (10)	218
Daisy White (11)	218
Edward Brent (11)	219

Ryan Alexander, Ben Montgomery & Louis Thrumble (8)   220
Michael Karpathios (9)   220
Max Tomlinson (8)   221
Eleanor Brent (8)   221
Lucy Stansbury (9)   222
Rory Atkins (9)   222
Georgia Beatty (9)   223
Annaliese Dillon (9)   223
Martha Owen (8)   224
Joseph Jackson (8)   224
Joseph Whittall (8)   225
James McLennan (9)   225
Oscar Addis (9)   226
Sam Norman (9)   226
Georgia Skinner (10)   227

The Cedars Primary School
Satvinder Khangoora (9)   227
George Baker (9)   228
Jordan Anthony (10)   228
Nadia Medjkoun (8)   228
Philip Hook (10)   229
Ryan Wilkinson (10)   229
Kamilha Imran (8)   229
Ryan Warner (8)   230
Marcus Row (9)   230
Luis Velaquez (7)   230
Thomas McKenna (10)   231

Twickenham Preparatory School
Ciara Spencer (10)   231
Claire Leslie (10)   232
Gordon Parker (10)   232
Amy-Ciara Turner (11)   233
Jasmine Pastakia (10)   233
Imogen Thain (10)   234
Harriet Page (9)   234
Hayley Dixon (10)   235
Lloyd Allen (11)   236
Sarah Hopkin (10)   237
Andrew Home (11)   238

Matthew Born (9)	238
Chloe Gale (10)	239
Gwen Owen Jones (9)	240
Holly Louise Squires (8)	240
Fleur Kenny	241
Zoë Monckton (10)	241
Charlotte Matten (10)	242
Amy Horrell (9)	242
Florence Brady (10)	243
Rupi Thind (8)	243
Taran Hothi (9)	244
Emily Jordan (9)	244
Cameron Sumner (9)	245
Isabelle Manning (9)	245
Francesca Harland (10)	246

The Poems

Earth

The planet Earth is everyone's home
It's where we live
We build our nests, huts and houses
In meadows.
The planet Earth is a free world
With food, money, toys, cars, pets, sweets
The planet Earth is as big as the sun
In summer it's hot
In spring daffodils grow
In autumn plants lose their leaves
And sleep for a whole season.

Amir Amraie (10)

Negative

Swirling wind in her face,
How can she help having her race?
Deserted, alone. Can she fit in . . . ?
They're throwing her patient words in the bin,
It's a hurtful kind.
How can we find
The place where people will be
In harmony?

She imagines a different kind,
Not alone she can step inside
A place that feels fun, fit in
Come and help
A stressing desire.
'Hi come over,' not, 'liar, liar.'

Peace and hope, we need today
So shall we live in a different way?

Haaniah Hamid (9)
Alexandra Junior School

Seasons Come And Go . . .

Winter comes with snow,
Weather changes in days to come . . .

Spring is *here!* with the smell of fresh air
And families are together.

Summer has *fun!*
With holidays to come.

Autumn is sad, families go
And never come *back!*

It's really heartbreaking because people die
Throughout those seasons . . .

So let's enjoy the fun.

Gurinder Rayat (9)
Alexandra Junior School

Untitled

There's a monster under my bed
But he didn't say said.
So he went to school
But he wasn't cool,
So he went home
But he had grown.
His mum saw his face,
She started to moan,
So I helped him,
I felt sad for him, so I did
And from that day on he helped me.

Manraj Ubhi (8)
Alexandra Junior School

I Need Help

I am bony and flexible,
I will tell you what I have been dreaming . . .
I have washed away to shore,
I have gazed over windows.
I have turned to ice all the way through,
I am shivering all the way to Earth around and around,
Let me have a cup of tea before I go,
Help me!

Hema Gautam (9)
Alexandra Junior School

My Brother

My brother is as storming as a giant.
He swarms here and there for trouble,
He pops all my bubbles.
My brother is a pain in the neck.
He is like a panting pirate on his deck.
He is like a monster on his dreadful duty,
He hates sensitive Sleeping Beauty.

Yasmin Khatri (9)
Alexandra Junior School

My Friends

My friends are kind and caring,
Whenever I am sad
They cheer me up.
They are such great fun,
I like my friends a lot.

Harpreet Phull (8)
Alexandra Junior School

Animal Cruelty

Leopards and elephants, tigers and fish,
They never do well on a dinner dish.
Animal cruelty is not so fair,
Even if it is a little polar bear.
You might like wearing animal fur,
But that won't make your little kitten purr.
If it's you that's giving out animal cruelty,
You should think before you feel so guilty.

Sian Bhatti (9) & Caitlin Seaman
Alexandra Junior School

The Sea!

My sea is bright,
But not light.
My sea is kind,
But not fine.
My sea is warm but not cold,
My sea has dolphins but no sharks.
My sea has shine but not light,
Swish, swash, swish, swash, swish, boo!

Sehar Mir (8)
Alexandra Junior School

My Dogs

I like my dogs,
They are wicked
But they also are really pretty.
I play with them,
I love them so much,
They are my dogs
And they are strong.

Wiktoria Wiszenko (9)
Alexandra Junior School

My Pet Cloe

My pet's name is Cloe
And she's very, very snowy.
Her eyes are black
Like really black bats.

Her paws are sharp
Like the teeth of a shark
And she's only 2 years old.

I love her so, so much
And she can make such a fuss
And everyone would like to have her.

My next-door neighbour
Gives her food
If she's in a nice mood!

She's never in her life had a fight,
And never, never, never has been out at night.

Priyanka Jethwa (8)
Alexandra Junior School

Mr Brain!

My pet's name is Mr Brain
And he has a big fat foot,
So he can't fit in the drain,
His leg is in a hook!

He is insane
'Cause he sits on a book
Without going on the crane,
Whenever he bangs the train,
He blames Mr Cook!

Whenever he sits he plays a game
With a look!

Rima Shah (8)
Alexandra Junior School

Super Shop

Fed up with your old bed?
Well that's no problem,
Come to our shop, the super shop,
We'll give you the comfortable bed
Which you will like and you
Will feel like you can stay on
It forever and ever and ever.
It's not that much money
Just £155.
You know you want one,
We asked some of our customers,
First we asked Mrs Giggle Miare,
She giggled and said,
'This is the best bed in the world,
So *get it!'*

Srishti Neogi (9)
Alexandra Junior School

Chocolate Land

Go to Chocolate Land
And you will go mad.
Every volcano splutters melted choc',
It really, really rocks.
Taste each sort of chocolate, plain, milk and dark,
But don't forget white, it really is a mark.
But go there early,
it's getting melty.

I can't believe it,
Can you?
It sounds weird,
Don't you think?
A chocolate land!
A chocolate land!

Yasmine Mansouri
Alexandra Junior School

My Poem About The Haunted House

The haunted house is rather horrible,
Rather spiky, rather terrible,
Never enter or you'll die in vain,
You should just leave it in lonely pain.

Creeping ivy going through the cracks of windowpanes,
The jet black paint peeling off the doors,
Just like 50 years so long, long ago,
No person lives there,
No car belongs there.

There was a brave lady who had lots of courage,
She entered and fought as much as she could,
But there was no point to enter inside
Because her flesh got stuffed and turned into stew,
But after a while the door flew open and scattered her bones.
The story's been passed from generations,
But that's for now my foes.

Priya Gupta (9)
Alexandra Junior School

My Dog Charlie

Fluffy brown fur like a leopard's coat,
He runs as fast as a speedy boat.
The patch on his ear is as white as a pearl,
He is a boy and he's not a girl.

He's the best dog anyone could have, I say,
He runs around almost every day.
The soles of his feet are jet black,
I told him to sit and he actually sat.

Charlie is the best thing in my life,
He is too young so he doesn't need a wife.
I love him so much, he's my best friend,
I hope it will last and never ever end.

Sian Bhatti (9)
Alexandra Junior School

Socks

I am fed up with your socks,
They are as fat as rocks.
They don't suit you at all,
You should get them thinner then they will be better,
I hate your socks.

Whenever you wear them you look fat,
You really look like a pig, don't wear them.
The socks are as stripy as a zebra,
Oh dear it does not suit you.

Oh what shall I do? You have stripy socks,
You wear them in bed and never take them off.
You should take them off,
Or I will go.

You will never get in the house
If you don't take off your stripy socks,
They are too smelly
Because you don't take care of them.

Ifia Chaudhri
Alexandra Junior School

I'm Sailing Out To Sea

I'm sailing out to sea,
Then I saw a bumblebee
Who looked at me.

I'm sailing out to sea,
I swam to a flea,
I jumped on a toilet to have some privacy.

I wrote down the number two,
Then I jumped in the loo,
Then I said, 'Boo!'

Wajidur Rahman
Alexandra Junior School

My Flower

My flower is pretty red,
My flower has pretty petals,
All the bees love it.
I'm sure it's great,
I keep my flower nice and clean
Because I give it sun and cream.
I love my flower so much,
I will never leave it out of my sight.

Christine
Alexandra Junior School

Sunny Day

A swift sun came
Like an alien dame.
As a spaceship tipped
The sun was clipped.
Hot heat when are you gone?
In hot heat you will moan.

Kaiya Adams
Alexandra Junior School

Jack's Adventure

Jack went to sleep, then he woke up,
He saw a giant beanstalk.
He climbed up the beanstalk,
He saw a castle and he went in,
He saw lots of food.

Khezer Ismail
Alexandra Junior School

Eating Chocolate

I was gobbling chocolate
And it was really yummy.
I ate too much, I had a bad tummy,
I got so fat like a balloon,
That I nearly floated to the moon.

My cousins stole some
And thought it was yucky,
They started to run around the room
Like a Loony Toon.
We went to the doctors
And he said, 'I have to give you medicine
For a lot of reasons.'

I had the medicine,
Then I had more problems,
I had to go to the doctors again.
Before, the doctor had said the wrong thing,
He'd said 3 times a day
But he meant to say ten times a day.

Harvir Ubhi
Alexandra Junior School

Baby Numbers

I'm number 1, let's have some fun.
I'm number 2, how do you do.
I'm number 3, would you play with me?
I'm number 4 and I can't take this anymore.
I'm number 5, there is no beehive.
I'm number 6, there won't be a mix.
I'm number 7, I feel like I'm in Heaven.
I'm number 8, there will be a big debate.
I'm number 9, there is no Frankenstein.
I'm number 10, I like Big Ben.

Shahzain Syed
Alexandra Junior School

Power Cut

A big loud thunder came through my ear,
I clutched the curtain with a lot of fear!
It came closer to my house,
I could not even hear a mouse!

Mum came into my room
And asked me if I had seen the broom!
Mum it's not the time for jokes,
Come on Mum, you're my folks!

I was beginning to get weak,
The water inside me began to leak!
The power went out,
I began to shout!

Mum wanted to make tea
But instead she has ice coffee!
We tried to ring
A man called Ping.

The next bright sunny morning
There was a kind of warning,
Still no power,
But only for one hour.

Balpreet
Alexandra Junior School

The Whale

Fierce bursting blow hole,
Gigantic as a thousand bowls,
Black and white camouflaging skin,
Can you catch that enormous thing?

Black, white, blue and grey,
Killer whales are coming today.
Can you see his razor-sharp teeth?
I don't know I think that's a fish.

Matteo
Alexandra Junior School

The Wizard

There was a wizard who lived down the lane,
He was such a big pain.
I went across to his house,
All I could hear was a mouse.

There was a wizard who lived down the lane,
While we were doing our homework he went insane,
And it started to rain,
It was a big nightmare.

There was a wizard who lived down the lane,
There isn't a wizard who doesn't live down the lane.

Aleesha Toor (9)
Alexandra Junior School

The Worst Day

I went to see Haaris,
But he went to Paris.
I went to see Freddy,
But he was a teddy.
I went to the funfair,
But it was a nightmare.
Then I went to my home
And I gave a huge moan!

I went to the park,
But it was too dark.
I went to my mate's,
But it was too late.
I met a young man,
But it was my nan.
I went to my house,
I saw a big mouse!

Freddy Farias (9)
Alexandra Junior School

The Snow

I was going to town when I saw snow on my nose,
It was white from the sky, white as light.

I smelt the snow, it smelt like a freezing rose.
Hoping to see more snow I looked up high.

It was beautiful, it was like sunflowers coming down.
The snow was going because people's feet were on the ground.

Mateusz Kryba
Alexandra Junior School

PE Poem

Socks off. Jump!
Shorts on. Hop!
Just keep moving
Till I say stop!

Legs jog,
Arms bent.
Don't talk
To your friends!

Along the beam,
Don't fall!
Keep your balance,
Walk tall.

Climb the ropes,
Don't be slow.
To the top,
Up you go!

Well done,
That's really nice!
Now line up,
Quiet as mice.

Roda Hassan (9)
Alexandra Junior School

Perfect Peacock

There she goes twisting!
With a tip she arrives,
Hardly an ant can survive,
Her tail is colourful like a rainbow with dashes of ruby-red,
Dare to disobey and you won't see daylight.

There she goes twisting and twirling,
She says hi! But never flies!
Beak as orange as the sparkly sun,
She is the queen so don't be mean,
Her feathers are blue and seaweed-green.

There she goes twisting!
I said don't be mean you ugly thing!
The tigers try to make a band to impress the land,
Narrows her eyes at all who see her,
They sparkle and shimmer . . .

So remember don't mess with a peacock.

Yasmin Chahal (9)
Alexandra Junior School

Out Of School

Out of school,
There was a pool.
I saw a fool
And he jumped into the pool.
I saw a crook
And he took
My hook.
I saw Goofy
And he called Spoofy.
I saw a lamb
And he went bam!

Alfaz Brepotra (9)
Alexandra Junior School

Volcano Voltage

A fountain of lava bursts,
Golden gems exploding out,
Rock black as coal,
People run about.

A fountain of lava bursts,
Bloodcurdling lava burns
Red as fire,
But it won't learn.

A fountain of lava bursts,
It's ashes falling like rain,
Tisel! Tisel! Tisel!
But it broke its chains.

Sidorela Gjeci (9)
Alexandra Junior School

The Poem

I am a pen,
I write in ink.
My friend is Ben,
He eats the hen.
My mum is called Jen,
She is more than ten.

I am a pen,
I've been coloured.
My friend is cuddled
Up by a pencil case,
He is kind.
My mum had been folded on a paper,
She is more than ten.

Nikita Mehtaj
Alexandra Junior School

Rainforest

In the rainforest it all began,
The buildings, cities,
Cosy cottages,
Even a huge shopping mall,
Rainforest, you did it!

In the rainforest it all began,
Beautiful beaches and lovely sand gold as the sun,
Exciting get aways which are good and fun!
I didn't eat fish or animals but fruit.

Jasdeep Kaur Bansal (8)
Alexandra Junior School

The Crocodile

His skin is green and bumpy.
His eyes are small and scary.
His skin is rough and hard.
His teeth are like knives.
His feet are like witches' hands.
His mouth is like a peg.

Gin
Alexandra Junior School

Sharks

Sharks have sharp teeth,
Sharks eat stale beef,
Sharks have a swimming kit,
Sharks are very fit,
Sharks have a clasp which is very fast.

Jae Letch (9)
Alexandra Junior School

Problem Page

Dear Morren,
I'm a fountain pen.
Every day somebody's grubby little hand takes my head off
And drags my brain across a piece of paper
As white as a pearl,
But as rough as varnished wood.
Sometimes they bend the tip of my brain
And some day it might vanish!
Gone! Gone! Gone!
From your dear friend, Fountain Pen.
PS - Help me! Help me! Help me!

Sarandeep Kaur Judge (9)
Alexandra Junior School

Untitled

I went to my friend's,
When I saw him,
I shook his hand,
He was fresh, I was cool.
We decided to watch,
His mum made good tea,
We had cookies and cake
And we were feeling great.

Zeeshan Deen (8)
Alexandra Junior School

My Family Is Sleeping Late

My family is sleeping, I want my mum to wake up.
Wake my mum up, oh no my mum is sleeping late today.
It's time to go to school, oh the head teacher is gonna
Shout at me because I'm late.

Frankie Romp
Alexandra Junior School

Fed Up With Your Old Skateboard!

Fed up with your old skateboard!
Buy a new powered skateboard!
It has all inventions you like,
It is so *cool* because you can go on walking.
It has a remote control so you don't have to move it with your legs.
It also contains a uniform and a helmet to keep you safe.

But beware it is attracted to metal,
If you get stuck push the button on your belt and you're free.

Premal Shah
Alexandra Junior School

Springtime

Juicy carrots from underground,
Rabbits waiting to dig the ground,
Mother duck had a new baby,
But she was too ugly to make friends.
The beautiful pond was full of ducks,
No more could fit on the pond.
Bees and butterflies looking for nectar,
All filled up, what a beautiful garden
To make new friends and meet new relatives.

Luca
Alexandra Junior School

The Ogre

Eyes are green and blue all over,
If you see him he'll beat you with a brick.
Legs are fluffy, long, they go far,
Makes me sick when I lick my lips.
His brain is like squidgy goo,
He makes me sick.

Dylan Angelidakis
Alexandra Junior School

The Castle

The dark house on the hill,
The rough hard, the weak one,
Dark at night standing upright,
They say it stands there for a fright.
People say it's fun.

The dark house on the hill,
The one like a rubbish bin inside,
Hopping like a frog round and round,
The one that wants to go on a ride,
It probably costs a few pounds.

Shuhada Khanom (8)
Alexandra Junior School

My Baby Sister

Amrit is my baby sister,
She is a clever clog,
She talks non-stop,
She jumps like a frog.

She copies me like a copycat,
She repeats like a parrot,
She is cheeky like a monkey,
She would love to chew a carrot.

She is a roly-poly,
Her hands are soft like marshmallows,
Her eyes are chocolate-brown,
Her favourite colour's yellow.

I love my baby sister,
She's naughty but nice,
Her favourite dish is curry and rice.

Indpal Kaur Kullar (10)
Andrew Ewing Primary School

Families

I love my mum,
I love my dad,
My brother and sister
Just drive me mad.

We do things together,
We do things alone,
We have great fun
When we're at home.

We go to the beach,
We go to the zoo,
We scare all the animals
When we say boo!

We have a pet,
His name is Jack,
He's only a goldfish,
How funny is that?

I like my school,
I love my weekends,
That's when I play
With all my friends.

Then I go to sleep,
I turn out the light,
My mum tucks me in
And Dad says, 'Goodnight!'

At the end of the day, it's plain to see,
That everyone needs a family!

Ricky Garcha (10)
Andrew Ewing Primary School

Why Is It Always Me?

Why is it always me
Who is full of hopes and dreams,
But yet they never come true?
I try and try my best,
I try harder than the rest,
I try - I really do!

Shall I tell you what I want to be?
Alright! Listen carefully!
I really want to be a poet,
I am really good at it,
My mind is really fit,
I would pass as a poet - I know it.

Guess what? I have learnt how to write!
My standards have gone up a flight,
I am also a professional poet,
I have written books and books,
Talent was all it took.
As for my talent - I will show it!

That is the end of my story,
To my major step to glory,
I would like to take this moment to say thanks;
To everyone who stood by me,
Although I did the work, really!
I did!

Jasmine Kaur Pank (11)
Andrew Ewing Primary School

Haunting

Ghosts, ghosts in the darkness of the night,
Ghosts, ghosts in the ghost train.
Ghosts, ghosts giving you a fright,
Ghosts, ghosts they give you a pain.

Frankenstein and his ugly face,
Frankenstein smells really bad.
Frankenstein looks a disgrace,
Frankenstein can make you sad.

Mummies are Egyptian,
Mummies can scare.
Mummies aren't fiction,
Mummies are here so beware!

Monsters' favourite things are food,
Monsters are really bad.
Monsters are always in a bad mood,
Monsters can get really mad.

Shivam Bansal (11)
Andrew Ewing Primary School

Snooker

It all started at the Masters,
Where John Parrot predicted disasters,
John Parrot caught the flu,
So what could he do?
Rocket Ronnie potted too many,
As he broke his cue
Out of the blue.
John Parrot ate a carrot,
So he could play too!
Paul Hunter needed this frame,
Otherwise he was going to lose the game,
When John Parrot beat Rocket Ronnie,
He also received a lot of money!

Gautam Tankaria (10)
Andrew Ewing Primary School

My Brother

His cheeks are as soft as pillows,
His feet are the size of marshmallows,
His smile is as cheerful as can be,
He is so precious to me.

He wears such cute little clothes
And has very tiny toes,
When he's wrapped in his shawl
He looks so cuddly and small.

I'm happy when he's awake
Because I can play.
I wish I could see him
Every moment of the day.

He is my little baby brother,
To me he is like no other.
He was born on New Year's Day
And now he is here to stay.

Bavneet Kaur Aulakh (11)
Andrew Ewing Primary School

The Strange Zoo

One day I went to the zoo and saw . . .

A lion that was scared
And a monkey that just stared.

A giraffe that was short
And a tiger that never fought.

An elephant that was small
And a snake that could crawl.

And at the end they put me in the zoo
And said, 'You're mad too.'

Simran Kaur Kahlon
Andrew Ewing Primary School

Camping

Another year, another camp,
What will it be this time?
Will it be sunny or will it be rainy?
I should know I am brainy,
Will there be slugs or will there be rats?
Hopefully there are no bats.

Another year, another camp,
What will we do this time?
Will we go climbing, caving or hiking?
Who knows, we might go biking,
Will we sleep early or will we sleep late?
I hope I sleep next to my mate.

Another year, another camp,
What will we eat this time?
Will it be cream or will it be custard?
I hope there is no mustard,
Will there be hot chocolate or will it be tea?
Oh look, a drink for me.

This camp will be the best this year
And everyone will give a great cheer!

Charlotte Richardson (10)
Andrew Ewing Primary School

2004!

2004 is here,
Enjoy the days that it shows,
Before you blink your eyes, it will go,
So just enjoy the days it shows.
Soon you will be waving goodbye to 2004,
Let's enjoy the days before they all fly,
But 2004 is new to us, we all just play out in the sun,
Now's the day to go to the beach because in the cold
We will have to sit inside and watch the rain fall,
So let's enjoy the days as they all go by.

Pavandeep Kaur (11)
Andrew Ewing Primary School

My Family

I've got a little family,
We live together happily,
Well!
Not exactly.

I've got a little brother,
He's so much of a bother,
I feel like kicking him out of the house,
Or maybe turning him into a mouse.

I've got a horrible big sister,
She comes on to me like a twister,
She is as smelly as a rotten cat
And is as stinky as a bat.

Now to my mummy,
She's so funny,
She has a big fat tummy
And eats sweet honey.

I've got a daddy,
He's such a baddy,
He drinks a lot,
A beard he's got.

Finally, my uncle Ben,
He looks after a hen,
He's as big as a hot air balloon,
You see, he's born in June.

I know it's a funny little family.

Bushra Nasim (10)
Andrew Ewing Primary School

The Seasons

Autumn
The kids are playing,
The trees are swaying,
A ripple of red and gold.
The leaves are falling, the sun is stalling,
The birds fly south from the cold.
Trees are bare, no one cares,
The central heating goes on.
The start of the football season gives me the reason
To meet all my mates in the park.

Winter
We may get some snow, nobody knows
If it will ever arrive.
Crisp and white, then sleet and ice,
Off we go to play.
Wrapped up warm, against the storms,
Santa's on his way. Mince pies and Christmas pud,
All on Christmas Day.

Spring
The sun is here and so is spring,
Sunflowers bloom and hummingbirds sing,
Poppies and daffodils everywhere
And lots of flowers that will make you stare.
Go to the park and have some fun
For spring is here, enjoy the sun.
Every day we get so hot because we run about a lot.
Spring is here, spring is here.

Summer
The summer is hot every day,
Heated up by golden rays.
Every year, the same old cheer
Comes from schools on the last day of term,
So hip, hip hooray the summer holidays are here,
I'm off on a trip, see you next year.

Tomas James Dyerson (11)
Andrew Ewing Primary School

I'd Like To Be . . .

I'd like to be a butterfly
Flying through the sky,
Going flower to flower
Each and every hour.

I'd like to be a cat
Dozing on the mat,
Always trying to catch a mouse
And bring it back to my house.

I'd like to be a rattlesnake
And try to bake a cake,
I'd hunt my prey
And my class is Marine Bay.

I'd like to be a dog
And go and fetch a log,
I'd run into the park
And bark and bark and bark.

I'd like to be a racing horse
And win every race,
I'd run on all the courses
And play against my friends.

Taylor Rowlands (10)
Andrew Ewing Primary School

Freedom

Freedom is good,
A blessing to us,
We take it for granted
Like a teddy's warm fuzz.

I hope you can feel
That warm little glow,
That is the freedom
That will never let go.

Jacob Hamblin-Pyke (9)
Archdeacon Cambridge's CE Primary School

Hallowe'en Night

Dark night,
Scary flight,
Yummy sweets,
Long beats,
Super suits,
High heel boots,
Long hats,
Flying bats,
Colourful lights,
Fun sights.

Cecilia Rose McCormick (8)
Archdeacon Cambridge's CE Primary School

Who Am I?

Fast swimmer,
Eye dimmer.
Fish swallower,
Boat follower.
Great jumper,
Huge thumper.

Alice Coaker Basdell (9)
Archdeacon Cambridge's CE Primary School

French People

Snail eaters,
Frog swallowers,
Wine gulpers,
Strange speakers,
Some are small and some are bigger,
Horrid singers,
Dirty geysers,
They look like each other.

Sam Foley (8)
Archdeacon Cambridge's CE Primary School

Leopard Kennings

Fast creature
Spotty feature
Brill climber
Fine mimer
Savage killer
Scare filler
Speedy runner
Supper cunner
Killer predator.

Craig Henry (8)
Archdeacon Cambridge's CE Primary School

School

Being bored to death,
Another word for prison.
A place where people teach us what we know.
A detention non-stop
And if everyone enjoyed this torture they would be mad!
A place where people sleep in every lesson,
Being forced to learn everything they say.

Jenanne Soboh (8)
Archdeacon Cambridge's CE Primary School

What Am I?

As big as a book.
As small as a bee.
As thin as a pencil.
As tall as a piece of paper.
As nice as a dog.
As good as you.

Peter Gorbutt (9)
Archdeacon Cambridge's CE Primary School

Bomb

Danger killer,
Red alert,
Life stealer,
Cruel, mean.
Explodes the scene,
Blood spiller,
Death filler,
Mega killer,
Loud speaker,
People seeker.

Elliott Morley (8)
Archdeacon Cambridge's CE Primary School

What Am I?

Car racer
Big facer
Pole winner
Getting thinner
Always first
Coming best
King basher
Big crasher.

Jeremy Laing (8)
Archdeacon Cambridge's CE Primary School

TV Kennings

Square screen
Big advertiser
Square eyes
Comedy box.

Elliot Tomos Webb (8)
Archdeacon Cambridge's CE Primary School

The Sea

Glittering glimmery top,
Down in the water is a shop.

Sandy glow from the bottom,
Little fishes do a show.

As blue as the sky,
Every fish has a sharp eye.

A home for glowing fish,
Everyone is going.

Terrific turquoise glinting in the sun,
All the sharks are having a fish bun.
Yum, yum.

Molly Purdue-Guy (8)
Archdeacon Cambridge's CE Primary School

The Shark

Fierce fighter
Raging blighter
Man basher
Fish smasher
Tail swisher
Angry fisher
Rock breaker
Man baker
Fish masher
Boat trasher.

Jessica Pead (8)
Archdeacon Cambridge's CE Primary School

What Am I?

Man eater
Raging beater.

Burning shredder
Murder spreader.

Life stopper
Jungle topper.

Roaring king
Amazing sting.

Really fast
Just a blast.

Oliver Foudah (9)
Archdeacon Cambridge's CE Primary School

What Am I?

All rhyming
Perfect timing
Never stops
Get them in shops
Writing time
Must be in line
On the board
Can't get bored
In the book
Take a look!

I am a poem.

Meg Riley (8)
Archdeacon Cambridge's CE Primary School

The Jet Plane

A big fright
A huge height
A stunt spinner
A race winner
A fast thing
A small wing
Extremely fast
Exciting blast.

John Stanley (8)
Archdeacon Cambridge's CE Primary School

The Sea

Gorgeous, greeny blue
Shimmering surface
Sandy bottom
Chattering mad
Crashing madly
Shimmering crazy
Shiny topping
Slim swimming.

Emilia Marshall (8)
Archdeacon Cambridge's CE Primary School

Guess Who I Am?

Sweet smeller,
Future teller,
Pink heather,
Grows together,
Love maker,
Personality shaker,
Garden habitat.

I am a rose.

Charlotte Kelsted (9)
Archdeacon Cambridge's CE Primary School

Car

Bumpy ride
Soft inside.

Door banger
Wheel clanger.

Tyre roller
Round bowler.

Motor screecher
Wheel preacher.

Stephanie Knight (9)
Archdeacon Cambridge's CE Primary School

Who Am I?

Mud chaser
Filth maker.

Net shredder
Ball setter.

Leg sneaker
Boot seeker.

Song singer
Speedy winger.

Michael Oliver Capon (9)
Archdeacon Cambridge's CE Primary School

The Sun

Ice melter
Beach maker
Hot summer
Person heater
Light brighter.

Albert Ewin (9)
Archdeacon Cambridge's CE Primary School

Who Am I?

Road blocker,
Noise rocker.
Big toy,
Loves boys.
Moves cement around,
Rolls on ground.
Helps with roadworks.

I am a cement mixer.

Ria St Hilaire (9)
Archdeacon Cambridge's CE Primary School

Fish

Shiny scales,
Never fails,
Jumps high,
Never flies,
Flap, spin,
Got to win.
Great style,
Swim a mile.

Clarissa Jeffery (9)
Archdeacon Cambridge's CE Primary School

Worm

Slimy thing
Wriggly ring
Pink hair
Very bare
Alive creature
Wise teacher
Garden preacher.

Louise Breckon (9)
Archdeacon Cambridge's CE Primary School

School

Learning habits
No rabbits
Working daily
Meeting Haley
Homework giver
Weekly liver
Horrid dinners
Loads of sinners
Horrid science
With Mr Flyence.

Matthew Harris (9)
Archdeacon Cambridge's CE Primary School

What Am I?

I am something slimy
With different patterns.
Keep away or I'll bite
And give you fright.

A snake.

Raad Begh (8)
Archdeacon Cambridge's CE Primary School

One Night

One night I had a strange dream,
It made me scream.
I saw a hand stuck to the wall,
It was holding a ball.
I said to the hand, 'Give me the ball,
You've got to stop.'
Good job my mum came
And woke me up!

Dariush Salek (8)
Ashton House School

Winter Poem

There is a lovely sparkling sight
Down the street and in the night.

We are playing, laughing, having fun,
Joy and wonder have just begun.

Autumn leaves have fallen to the ground,
No leaves are seen or none are found.

The winter season's fresh, cool breeze
Blowing and swaying the lifeless trees.

Soon the snow falls all around,
Falling swiftly to the ground.

Whitening and softening your green grass,
Treading on it as you pass.

Radheka Agarwal (9)
Ashton House School

Liking The Weather

I really do not know why people don't like snow,
It's cold and white and crunchy and bright.
It sparkles like diamonds in the sun
And covers the branches like icing on a bun.
I really do not know why people don't like snow.

I really do not know why people complain about rain,
It's wet and watery, clear and clean.
It glistens on spiders' webs in the sun
And jumping in puddles is really good fun.
I really do not know why people complain about rain.

But what everyone likes best, and I also agree
Are the days that are dry, warm, bright and sunny.

Harry Bourne (9)
Ashton House School

How Spring Begins

Bluebells swaying in the breeze,
Brightly coloured crocuses bloom with ease.
Clusters of snowdrops scattered around,
Yellow daffodils sprouting from the ground.

The stubby primrose bold and bright,
Scented hyacinths stretching for the light.
Tissue paper blossom pink and white,
Soft and delicate - what a pretty sight.

Clumps of purple violets drinking the morning dew,
The dawn sky with a delightful blue hue.
Blankets of buttercups sitting in the sun,
These are the signs that spring has just begun!

Natalie Watts (10)
Ashton House School

Best Friends

My best friend is so special to me,
She makes me laugh out loud you see.
We spend as much time as we can together,
Walking and playing in all sorts of weather.

At school we sit as close as we can,
Our talking and chatting can get out of hand.
All through playtime you'll never see us apart,
Unless one of us is ill and we're like a spare part.

It's very important to have good friends,
With who you can share secrets and always depend.
As I grow up I will always remember
My very best friend, friends forever.

Emily Ann Watson (10)
Ashton House School

A Wish

Annie wishes to live in Disneyland,
Where in parades there are marching bands.

Autographs she will get
And all characters
She will not forget.

She will go on all the rides
And time will pass by
So quickly that she will not realise.

Her favourite show she will see
And happily pretend to be
Princess Ariel in the sea.

Winter will be wonderful
With all those fireworks in the sky.

Summer will be hot and busy
But that will not stop Annie
From seeing her friends,
Minnie and Mickey.

Iman Jasani (9)
Ashton House School

There's A Fire In The Forest

Help! Help! There's a fire in the forest,
The animals are scared.
The flames are fierce,
The bushes are burnt
And the trees have fallen on the ground.
Oh! *No!* The ground. Help!

The fire has gone, everything is black and burnt.
There's just one plant left.
Hey, wait a minute, it's a magic plant,
The forest is back!
The wonder of nature.

Aaron Singh Saran (8)
Ashton House School

If I Could Be . . . I Would

If I could be anything . . .
I would be a goalie for NUFC.

Saving goals, punching away,
Looking to the left, looking to the right,
Clearing danger,
So no goals pass my line.

Diving across the face,
Stretching to the corners,
Kicking the ball away.

The feeling of the ball
In my hand,
Saving my team
From being banned.

The match has finished,
We have won,
That's another glorious day I've done.

I go home on cloud nine,
I then wake up, it's all in my mind.

If I could be . . . I would.

Waseem Sayid (11)
Ashton House School

Funky Josh

F unky Josh!
U nusual Josh,
N obody can help laughing.
K arate Josh,
Y ippee!

J osh is clever,
O h
S o cool!
H ave you met him?

Josh Thakrar (8)
Ashton House School

The Magician

The magician of ambition
Caused a nuclear collision,
Then he made his own decision
To say sorry to the nation.

His brain was telepathical
And was truly acrobatical.
He got a bit practical
But he was never ever tactical.

He always did revision
Of addition and division,
But don't forget his favourite,
Long multiplication.

The magician's true ambition
Was successfully fulfilled
Thanks to the transmission
On national television.

Umair Mughal (11)
Ashton House School

My Dog Chewed Up My Homework!

I'm glad to say my homework's done,
I finished it last night.
I've got it right here in this box,
It's not a pretty sight.

My dog chewed up my homework,
He slobbered on it too,
So now my work is ripped to shreds
And full of slimy goo.

It isn't much to look at
But I brought it anyway,
I'm going to dump it on your desk
If you don't give me an A!

Jaipal Sachdev (10)
Ashton House School

Friendship

Friendship is very, very unique
And it is something,
Something that we all should seek.

You need a friend to talk to in life,
A friend to whom we can go to
In times of stress and strife.

A friend who's always near
And there throughout the years.
A friend we know will care
And take away our fears.

If you do not have a friend
You will be bored and lonely,
But if you do have a friend
You will always feel very happy and homely.

Friendship is a priceless gift
That cannot be bought or sold.
Its value is far greater than
A mountain or a heap of gold.

Gold does not have life,
Nor a heart to understand.
It cannot give you comfort,
Or lend a helping hand.

So if you have a chance to ask God for anything
Then ask for a good friend.

Ruchit Gupta Chaudhary (11)
Ashton House School

Parents' Evening

We're waiting in the hall,
My mum, my dad and me.
They are sitting there talking,
Not nervous at all.
I wonder what she'll tell them,
I'll say I've got a nose bleed.
I wish I'd got my maths right,
I wish I had a brain.

We're waiting in the hall,
My wife, son and me.
My son is shaking,
I'm staring, nervously.
I hate coming to parents' evening,
What they do is make me fret.
They talk about my son
And then they are done.

We're waiting in the hall,
My husband, son and me.
I wonder what she'll tell us,
I hope it's not all bad.
He is a good boy,
But is lazy like his dad.

Waiting, waiting, waiting,
The teacher calls us in,
Looking very angry
With her red rosy cheeks,
She gives us a crisp white paper
With a big A
Which made our day.

Priya Grewal (11)
Ashton House School

Animal Poem

A little rabbit happily hopping around,
Is there anything to eat on the ground?
Hey, hey, hey! Give us some food,
A yummy carrot, some lettuce, anything to soothe my mood.

A happy dog playing in the sun,
Jumping about and having plenty of fun.
Come here my faithful little canine friend,
You and I will be together until the end.

A soft, little kitten cuddles and delights its mum,
What a loving, caring bond between mother and son.
Such beautiful, stunning blue eyes
And as all babies do, sometimes it cries.

Zaqi Ismail (11)
Ashton House School

Homework

The thing I hate most
When I come home from school
Is doing my homework,
Trust me, it is so not cool.

It might be fun in your school,
But definitely not in mine.
We get tons of it every day
And it takes such a long time!

I'd rather catch slugs
And put them in lines,
Than tackle the homework
My teacher assigns!

Khimi Grewal (11)
Ashton House School

Left In School

I look up from my desk,
I'm full of shock,
There's nobody there.
Where's everyone gone?

I run to the window,
There's no one out there,
When did they all go?
I didn't hear!

I look around the room,
It looks very bare,
There's nothing but tables and chairs,
It looks different when it's empty,
Now I'm feeling scared.

My heart's beating faster,
I've got butterflies in my tummy,
Oh dear, I think I want my mummy!

I walk out of the room to get my bag and coat,
They're the only ones there,
It's very quiet here.

All I can hear is tick-tock, tick-tock,
I look up and it's five o'clock.
I run out to the night,
School is over and I've been left behind!

Amanjai Sharma (11)
Ashton House School

Children's Day

5th of May,
I love this day
Because we get to play all day.

Don't go to school,
It's very cool
Because we get to play all day.

Invite our friends
To stay for tea,
To watch TV or DVD.

Go to the park
To meet some friends
And play fun games until this day ends.

This is why I love this day,
It's 5th of May,
It's a fantastic day!

MinWoo Park (9)
Ashton House School

Valentine's Day

Oh please, oh please,
Be my valentine,
I will love you until the end of life,
I will give you whatever you want,
My love, my life, my heart, my soul,
Anything that you will want.
I will always think of you and no one else,
You are the best and the only one,
For I always think about you and nothing else,
Oh please, oh please,
Be my valentine
And you will live the life you want.

Nishita Agarwal (9)
Ashton House School

I Am Your Friend

I live on this side of the world -
You live on the other,
I am just like you -
Boy or girl,
We may have a father and mother.

My country is strong,
My country is rich,
I eat well and sleep well,
You rummage for food in a ditch;
And I wonder what it would be like -
To be you;
Could I survive?

I am your sister,
I am your friend -
Take my hand,
Share my food;
In my mind I will send you best wishes,
For a good life and more,
And when the bombs fall in your streets,
I will protest -
Because you are weak
And you are poor,
Helpless children have so much more . . .
To offer the world . . .

Anique Joubert (9)
Ashton House School

Vegetables

I don't like vegetables
So I gave them to my cat,
My cat didn't like them
So I went away angry.

My mum said I had to eat them,
I already had tried my cat
So who to give them to?
I know, I'll try my bat!

So I gave them to my bat
Who was enjoying something,
He did not like vegetables,
He was eating a gnat.

I had no one to give them to,
So I threw them in the fire.
My mum said I ate them quickly
So she gave me a plateful more!

Hassan Qureshi (8)
Ashton House School

My Christmas Poem

C hurch bells are ringing,
H ouses are twinkling,
R oasters are steaming,
I vy is here to fill you with love and delight,
S anta is giving happiness to little ones,
T rees, Christmas trees, gleaming and full of delight,
M usical carols are being sung at this time of year.
'A ll's well that ends well.' It's a new year, a fresh start.
S apphires, turquoises and beautiful colours remind us of
the birth of Jesus.

Amal Ismail (12)
Aylward First & Middle School

I Know A Place

I know a place you can sit and dream
And nothing is as real as it seems,
Where you can fly around in the sky
And sit and watch the clouds go by,
Where anything is possible and as real as me and you,
But it only happens for a second or two,
Where nothing is wrong and everything is right
And it happens in my mind every day and every night.

Savannah Greenaway Bailey (11)
Aylward First & Middle School

Like A Monkey

I am like a monkey because . . .
I am very fun and energetic,
I swing from branch to branch,
I am the queen of the bananas,
You must think I am the best,
I am funnier than the rest,
I take the fruit from the ladies and the babies,
Everyone puts their hand up for me!

Ellen O'Brien (12)
Aylward First & Middle School

Christmas

C ome and join the celebrations!
H ave fun playing games.
R elax and have a good time.
I t's the giving, not the receiving.
S ing some Christmas carols.
T asty food for us to eat.
M any thanks for Christmas treats.
A nyone for Christmas pudding?
S anta is coming . . .

Gemma Kilkenny (12)
Aylward First & Middle School

Touching

Touching is an amazing thing,
You can feel almost anything,
Brick walls are strong and rough,
Leather is smooth and tough,
Glass is hard and shiny,
Butterflies are beautiful and tiny.

You can touch with your tongue,
Ice cream melts on it right away,
Ice-cold air on a winter's day,
Oranges, full of juice and zesty,
Bananas peeled, soft and squelchy,
Apples crunchy, so tasty in pastry,
All part of the taste-touching journey.

Touch is a wonderful thing,
The sense of touch can make your heart sing.
You can touch with your words,
Your heart and your mind,
Touch, soft, gentle and kind.

Bobby Bloch (10)
Aylward First & Middle School

Christmas Time

Christmas time is a loving time,
With presents to give and receive.
Be thankful and happy at this time
On this brightful day.

Christmas cards are flying around
With thanking for these gifts.
But people are kind and want a good time
For others and themselves.

Hailey Parker (12)
Aylward First & Middle School

Christmas Poem

Christmas night,
The sky is alight with twinkling lights,
Shiny and bright.
Warm houses,
Hot Christmas pudding,
Turkey sizzling in the oven.
Families unite, fires are bright,
It is Christmas night,
Merry Christmas,
With love, Hayley.

Hayley Wright (11)
Aylward First & Middle School

Anarchy

A violent scream!
N o law!
A terrifying place.
R idiculous,
C omplete disorder,
H ardly any heart,
Y ou should stay where you are safe.

Jessica Puplett (12)
Aylward First & Middle School

Anarchy

A town was not organised.
N o one knew what to do.
A ll the shops were looted.
R ioting was everywhere.
C oppers came along.
H auled everyone together.
Y ou'll all end up in the nick if you do it again.

Natasha Jayne Britton (12)
Aylward First & Middle School

The Violence In My City

When I walk down the street I see anarchy and pain
All of this violence drives people insane.

I see cars crashing, smoke in the air
I see blood and dead bodies everywhere.

When I watch the news I see a person that just died
The sad thing about it, is no one even cried.

If it was up to me everyone would live in peace
And all of this violence would eventually cease.

The truth is right before us if you look closely you can see
Why all of this bothers me.

All I need is a helping hand
To put a stop to this violence and take a stand.

All of this disaster sure isn't pretty
But that's how it is with the violence in my city.

Ahmed Adelabu (12)
Aylward First & Middle School

A Christmas Poem

Tonight it's snowing, children are playing,
Families are feasting with Christmas joy.
There are sweet sounds of Christmas lullabies around every corner.
It's said there are people that can't enjoy this joyous time
Because they are poor.
No Christmas pudding for you or for me,
No Christmas presents in our stockings,
But no! Just wait,
Saint Nick is on his way,
Maybe we will receive a present this joyful day.

Elizabeth Rose Bogue (11)
Aylward First & Middle School

Christmas

Christmas, Christmas, Christmas is coming,
Decorations are up, the robins are singing.
Tree lights flicker in the dark,
Along with the twinkling of the stars!

Christmas, Christmas, Christmas is coming,
Children are playing, the trees are swaying.
Snowmen are made and there they lie!

Christmas, Christmas, Christmas is coming,
There is not a sound and no one to be found.
Santa's coming, Santa's here delivering the presents everywhere.
Off on Rudolph he goes shouting, 'Ho, ho, *ho!*'

Christmas, Christmas, Christmas is *here!*
Gifts are opened.
Many happy faces are seen, in many different places.
'Hooray!' everyone shouts, Santa's come there's not a doubt!

Christmas, Christmas, Christmas is *not* here . . .
For the people who have no reason to cheer,
No home,
No care,
No love,
Shouting help, but no one listens, only the snowmen that melt.

Amélia Sheikh (11)
Aylward First & Middle School

Christmas Poem

Christmastime, the favourite time of the year,
it is time for happiness, not fear.
Children are excited, they cannot wait,
Playing outside with the snow, feeling great!
Get the heaters on, back door closed, it's getting cold!
People never get tired of Christmas, not even when they're old,
Christmas is not just about receiving, it's about giving too!
Don't be naughty! Just wait for Santa and his crew!

Dettori Shek (11)
Aylward First & Middle School

Christmas

C hrist is born,
H appy children smile,
R ushing to open the gifts,
I mpressed by the feast,
S tars glisten in the darkened sky,
T he colours of Christmas shine,
M erry Christmas!
A ngels sing in harmony,
S now falls.

Victoria Lewis (12)
Aylward First & Middle School

Christmas Time

Christmas time once again,
It started with a gift,
God loved the world,
He sent his son,
His only begotten son,
So that whoever believed in him,
Should have everlasting life.

Tahlia Theresa Lewington (11)
Aylward First & Middle School

The Christmas Tree

Green, glistening, glowing bright!
Red sparkling lights shine out,
Tinsel wings cover the tree,
Will it take a flight?
Led by its top-most star
Into the clear and crystal night.

Ayan Yussuf (11)
Aylward First & Middle School

Christmas

Christmas is a lot of joy,
Kids all wanting tempting toys,
Lots and lots of glistening stars,
Rosy faces as red as Mars,
Santa coming through the light,
Landing gracefully on rooftops white,
Everyone is fast asleep,
Santa's reindeers in a heap,
Creeping in all their homes,
Silently passing all the gnomes,
Putting presents under trees,
Making sure the kids don't see,
Then Santa goes away,
And all the kids begin to play.

Zainab Reza (11)
Aylward First & Middle School

All About Christmas

C is for the cold, red noses,
H is for the stockings hanging over the fireplace,
R is for the rosy faces,
I is for the icicles glittering, hanging off the railings,
S is for the snowmen melting outside houses,
T is for the twinkling, shiny stars,
M is for the magnificent colours of the gold ribbon on the presents,
A is for the angels with their glistening haloes,
S is for the sparkling frost.

All these things make Christmas special but not
As special as being with your family.

Rebecca Louise Varley (11)
Aylward First & Middle School

What Is Christmas

Christmas is a time of joy!
Christmas means spending time with
Your family and friends!
Christmas is a time of celebrating
The birth of baby Jesus!
Christmas is a time for singing
Christmas carols!
Christmas is a time for eating a
Special Christmas dinner!
Christmas is a time for decorating
Your house with festive lights!
Christmas is a time building a
Snowman!
Christmas is a time for opening gifts!

Nekhel Ramavrat (11)
Aylward First & Middle School

Christmas Tree

Christmas time is full of fun, of laughter,
Hope and joy.
Christmas time is toys and boys,
Playing in the snow.
Christmas time is bright and light,
With Christmas trees covered in bows.
Presents and love fill the room and
Warmth from the heart fills the eyes of
Little girls and little boys.
Christmas time is now here!
So, let's enjoy the fun and cheer!

Holly Jobling (12)
Aylward First & Middle School

Happiness Is . . .

Happiness is a friend that you can rely on and trust,
Happiness is the sun that shines brightly on you,
Happiness is a teacher that is beautiful and kind,
Happiness gives us pleasure when we help people,
When they first come to school.
Happiness is being in Heaven when the world is calm,
Happiness is being on the beach with your friends and family,
Because it is joyful and peaceful,
Happiness is when people remind you of when
You were in nursery,
Happiness is going exploring because it is fun
And you learn interesting things,
Happiness is a friend.

Chanelle Ellington (8)
Aylward First & Middle School

Christmas

Snow falling down like a rainfall
Washing the floor.
There is so much I can't open my front door,
The snow is like dust that you can see,
It's all over you and all over me,
There isn't a leaf on a tree.

Children throwing snowballs my way,
So I'm giving up my sorrows and decide to play.

Winter will end soon,
I hope it lasts past noon.

Sean Young (11)
Aylward First & Middle School

Science Happiness . . .

Happiness is fun in lessons because
You get to learn new things.
Happiness is football because we always win.
Happiness is smiling because it makes you happy inside.
Happiness is listening to classical music because it
Calms you down from a hard day's work.
Happiness is having a nice cool bath
Surrounded by bubbles.

Happiness is going to the beach because you
Can play in the sand which is fun.

Happiness is getting better at reading
Because you get to learn new words,
Happiness is when you are in Heaven relaxing,
Happiness is when you get to concentrate on your work,
Happiness is fun when you go to see your
Favourite rock band!

Lincoln Leech (7)
Aylward First & Middle School

Christmas Poem

Christmas, Christmas come and play,
Christmas, Christmas is the day,
Christmas is a time for giving,
Because of God, He made us living,
Let us all have joy and fun,
The day of Christmas has just begun.

God sent us light and love,
From the Heavens above,
Christmas, Christmas is the day,
Christmas, Christmas come and pray.

Jamie Edwards (11)
Aylward First & Middle School

Happiness

Happiness is playing with your friends,
Happiness is running after the football,
Happiness is making new friends,
Happiness is when you go outside,
Happiness is when you talk to your friends,
Happiness is when you eat chocolate,
Happiness is when you learn new things,
Happiness is when you go to the toilet,
Happiness is when you grow up and be a football player,
Happiness is when you draw stuff,
Happiness is when you see your friends,
Happiness is when you watch TV,
Happiness is when you get nice food,
Happiness is when you have lots of fun.

Sheiyaan Ahmed (8)
Aylward First & Middle School

Merry Christmas!

Merry Christmas!
Christmas is like a wish that came true,
Wish that helped all human kind.
Christmas has a warm feeling of its own,
Christmas is like the snow on a tree,
Christmas is like the star,
On top of a Christmas tree,
Christmas is like a present,
The excitement is great,
Christmas is in the heart of everyone,
Everyone loves Christmas.

Anam Soroya (12)
Aylward First & Middle School

Happiness Is . . .

Happiness is the way you can make
New friends and playing with my next-door neighbour.
Happiness is going swimming with everyone in the warm water.
Happiness is getting class stars and doing things together,
Happiness is going on holiday because we have fun!
Happiness is blowing out the beautiful candles on your birthday cake.
Happiness is eating lots of chocolates because it's yummy!
Happiness is going to the cinema and eating popcorn!
Happiness is doing my work because it is fun!
Happiness is playing in the snow because you
                             can make snowy things,
Happiness is eating fruit so you are healthy!

Lesley Warrington (7)
Aylward First & Middle School

I Know A Bedroom

I know a bedroom where the floor is tidy,
Where toys and the clothes are all away,
Quite dust free with a scented air freshener,
With sticky sweet wrappers in the bin,
There in the corner the bed lies,
Outside the window the birds fly,
A flower or two on the window side,
The wind blows in and cools the air,
Posters all sizes cover the walls,
That's my story of the bedroom I know.

Dawn Pearson (11)
Aylward First & Middle School

Happiness Is . . .

Happiness is going to the funfair because the rides are fast,
Happiness is going to the cinema,
Happiness is climbing trees,
Happiness is playing my Game Boy Advance,
Happiness is making snowmen because they're pretty,
Happiness is having family because you're cared for,
Happiness is going to a posh restaurant with family
                         because the food is nice,
Happiness is walking my dog because we have
                         adventures together.
Happiness is going on a plane because it's very
                         fast when it is taking off.
Happiness is having a water pistol fight with my dad
                         because it's exciting and fun.
Happiness is swimming in the cool sea
                         because the waves knock me over.
Happiness is sailing with Dad because it's very pretty,
Happiness is fishing with my grandad because we catch rare fish,
Happiness is when you get home from school and find out
Something wonderful has happened because it's a surprise,
Happiness is getting time to myself because no one bothers you,
Happiness is jumping about in the mud
And that's all that makes me happy.

Gavin Law (7)
Aylward First & Middle School

Happiness

Happiness is learning stuff you can learn,
Happiness is playing with stuff like playing on the snow,
Happiness is you can make some friends like playing with my Lego,
Happiness is blowing out candles because you are growing up,
Happiness is drawing because it is fun,
Happiness is going to the park because you're having fun.

Jonathon Lewington (8)
Aylward First & Middle School

Happiness

Happiness is a star because it shines so brightly in the beautiful sky,
Happiness is fun for you and for me,
Happiness is having fun with your friends,
Happiness is a smile on your face because it is fun,
Happiness gives us sweet dreams,
Happiness is going to bed because it is cosy,
Happiness is playing with my friends,
Happiness is getting a class star so we can have a class treat,
                         with my friends and the lovely teachers,
Happiness is staying at home with my family,
Happiness is going shopping so we can have food so we can live,
Happiness is coming to school so I can learn,
Happiness is when I am playing with my brothers in the garden,
Happiness is having a party because it is fun!

Dora Leaman (8)
Aylward First & Middle School

Happiness

Happiness is going swimming in warm water,
Happiness is playing on the beach in the wet sand,
Happiness is listening to ballet music because it
                         makes you feel joyful,
Happiness is going to school because you can
                         meet your friends,
Happiness is going to the zoo because you
                         can see all the different animals,
Happiness is going to a party because you can celebrate,
Happiness is going to church because you pray to God.

Michaela O'Brien (11)
Aylward First & Middle School

Happiness

Happiness is doing your homework
Because you enjoy doing it,
Happiness is playing with your friends
In the playground together,
Happiness is playing on the beach,
Happiness is eating your favourite meal
It makes you feel happy,
Happiness is looking after your mum and dad
When they are not well,
Happiness is having your birthday
You feel much older than before,
Happiness is cleaning up for your mum and dad
When you feel like it,
Happiness is going out with your friends
And having a girlie talk,
Happiness is printing out things on the computer
Because it makes you feel happy,
Happiness is playing computer games
With another so you are not alone,
Happiness is playing in the classroom with toys.

Riddhi Thakrar (7)
Aylward First & Middle School

Happiness

Happiness is getting new friends because you can play with them,
Happiness is getting better at drawing so you can draw neater,
Happiness is getting better at football so you can score goals,
Happiness is getting better at reading books so the teacher
                                                                  can be proud
Happiness is eating lots of chocolate because it is yummy,
Happiness is getting better at staying still because it is fun.

Happiness is helping each other.

Mohamed Mohamed (8)
Aylward First & Middle School

Happiness Is . . .

Happiness is fun because it gives you pleasure,
Happiness is a star because it's great,
Happiness makes us proud because you can make friends,
Happiness gives us a smile because we are happy,
Happiness gives delight and joy,
Happiness is going to school because it's fun,
Happiness is being friendly to a friend and sharing,
Happiness is becoming brilliant at your reading,
Happiness is sharing life with your family,
Happiness is someone you can rely on and trust.

Disha Patel (8)
Aylward First & Middle School

My Snowman

My snowman is big,
My snowman is fat,
My snowman is tall,
My snowman is silly,
My snowman is bold
And that's that.

Sam Marks (7)
Aylward First & Middle School

Happiness

Happiness is smiling at people,
Happiness is playing football because it's fun,
Happiness is having friends,
Happiness is golden time because it is funny,
Happiness is going swimming.

Zulfikar Zaffar (8)
Aylward First & Middle School

Happiness

Happiness is making new friends,
Happiness is having a family,
Happiness is reading by myself,
Happiness is going to school,
Happiness is getting a new job,
Happiness is watching a scary film,
Happiness is trying new food,
Happiness is having a birthday,
Happiness is celebrating Christmas time,
Happiness is painting a picture,
Happiness is having sisters,
Happiness is being good,
Happiness is having a new teacher,
Happiness is not getting hurt,
Happiness is going to parties,
Happiness is learning new things,
Happiness is doing sport,
Happiness is growing up,
Happiness is going to the movies,
Happiness is being together,
Happiness is playing games,
Happiness is playing in the snow,
Happiness is seeing new things,
Happiness is going to the beach.

Jordan Turner (7)
Aylward First & Middle School

Science

S cience is exciting,
C aterpillar turns into a butterfly,
I mmerse things in water and they will lose weight,
E ggs hatch into chickens,
N uts grow into trees,
C ondensation means rain,
E verything is science.

Kirsty Lewington (9)
Aylward First & Middle School

Happiness

Happiness is being together because you're not alone,
Happiness is learning new things because it's fun,
Happiness is having homework because you get to learn new things,
Happiness is having golden times because you get to play with toys,
Happiness is having a holiday because you get to sleep for
a long time,
Happiness is going to people's houses because you get to play
with them,
Happiness is going to the movies because you get to watch cartoons.

Hamzah Ahmed (8)
Aylward First & Middle School

Snow

Snow is cold,
Snow is white,
Snow is all over the world,
Snow is always fun to play with.

Snow is icy,
Snow is bright,
Snow is white on the Earth.

Snow is soft,
Snow is slippery,
Snow is wet,
Snow is here.

Jenisha Patel (8)
Aylward First & Middle School

Happiness

Happiness is when you spend time with your family,
Happiness is when I have chocolate,
Happiness is when I do my homework,
Happiness is when I play with my friends,
Happiness is when I don't get told off,
Happiness is when I go on holiday,
Happiness is when I go swimming in the swimming pool,
Happiness is when I go to my friend's house,
Happiness is when I watch TV with my friend.

Adam James (7)
Aylward First & Middle School

Happiness

Happiness is fun because you learn new
Things like science and literacy,
Happiness is playing in the playground,
I like rugby plus I like football,
Happiness is eating popcorn in the cinema,
Happiness is relaxing in your bed,
Happiness is playing races,
Happiness is watching Harry Potter.

Terrell Richards-Gayle (8)
Aylward First & Middle School

Light

Light, light
Shines so bright
Through the winters
Day and night.
Light, light
Is so bright
Keeps me warm
Through day and night.

Sophie Tan (8)
Aylward First & Middle School

Snow

Snow is cold,
Snow is white,
Snow is soft,
Snow is crispy,
Snow is cold, white, soft and crispy.

I make snowballs,
I play with snow,
I make a snowman,
I enjoy snowballs, snow and snowmen.

Donna Edwards (8)
Aylward First & Middle School

Mother's Day

Mother, mother,
She mutters about Mother's Day,
She'll bake and all she'll say,
'Misery, no such thing,'
She's all mine,
She says kind things about baby brothers,
She will lay and kiss me.
Mother's Day has come,
A marvellous day.

Saada Shuwa (8)
Aylward First & Middle School

It's Snowing Today

It's snowing today, what a wonderful sight,
But it's very icy, it gave my mum a fright,
I went outside to play,
We had a snowball fight,
We made a snowman as well,
Oh no, it's time for bed,
See you in the morning light.

Danielle Swift (8)
Aylward First & Middle School

Snow

I am happy,
I am happy,
Snow is here,
Snow is here,
Snow is white,
Snow is white,
Snowman is here,
Snowman is here,
I am happy,
I am happy.

Dean Davey (8)
Aylward First & Middle School

Football

Football is cool,
It's a little bit better than school,
Someone said to me, 'Look at that big fan,'
She's crazier than a shacked can,
Then I scored a goal,
The other team hit the pole,
They said, 'No goal,'
We said, 'At least we didn't hit the pole.'

Lewis Gray (7)
Aylward First & Middle School

Sun

Sun, sun you
Shine so bright,
You come in summer,
Why don't you in the winter?
Please come in the winter,
I like hot places.

Francesca Pagliaroli (7)
Aylward First & Middle School

Homework

Homework, oh homework!
I hate you,
You stink,
I could wrestle
A lion in the dark,
I could wash you
In the sink,
I could rip you
Up into bits,
Oh homework!
I am going to bed.

Mohammed Dedhar (8)
Aylward First & Middle School

Holiday In The USA

This holiday is the best,
Because there are
Lots and lots
Of rich people.
I like rich people
And ancient accents,
They're cool,
They have good food
Big cars and nice movies.

Kevin Da Mata (8)
Aylward First & Middle School

Snow Goes Down

When the snow goes down
And the sun goes away
I go and play
With a snowman that I've made
I have lots of fun playing in the snow.

Fiona Berbatovci (8)
Aylward First & Middle School

One Windy Night

One windy night the wind whistled
through the village of Cromby.
The snow began to fall which left a
blanket of snow on the roofs with tassels of snow dangling.
The only light in the village was coming
from the gold twinkling stars and the
full grey moon.
All the red from the roses had been taken over by snow.
All the yellow from the daffodils had
faded away into thin air, although
all the white from the daisies had
stayed right in place.
The wind whistled through the trees again
but the snow stayed on still ground.
It was one windy night to remember.

Abigail Ross (10)
Bishop Perrin School

Habitat

On a log sits a frog,
In the water lies a dog.

On the grass sits a rabbit,
In the trees, buzzing bees.

On the pond, a dragonfly,
In the sky, birds fly.

On the leaves, a caterpillar,
In the breeze I hear a quiver.

On a branch, a woodpecker,
Passing by, a double-decker.

Sophie Hopkins
Bishop Perrin School

Seasons

Summer, summer I love summer,
When it's winter, it's a bummer.

Winter, winter I hate winter,
Feels like a painful splinter.

Spring, spring I love spring,
It makes me want to sing, sing, sing.

In summer we have ice cream,
In winter we have no football team,
In spring we like to sing,
In autumn you can smell crackling.

I find no reason
That winter should be a season.

Robert Kirkham (10)
Bishop Perrin School

The Autumn Night

The wind whistled through the trees
as the sun slowly set in the distant sky.
Tree leaves blowing far away,
Rustled in the breeze.
The warmth of the evening sun made
the damp, wet ground steam.
The prickly hedgehog curled in a ball,
his spikes like the thorns of a rose bush.
An autumn blood-red sky melted into dark gloom,
Later in the evening, lights turn off for people to drift off to sleep.

Lydia Clarke (11)
Bishop Perrin School

Midnight

Every day when the clock strikes twelve
I wake up to take a peak outside
I don't know why and I don't know how,
Or when I started to wake at midnight.

The moon, it shines a bright light glow
A moonlight pillow, a blanket of stars
A bed to tuck the day away
To keep it warm, especially at midnight.

I see the fairies running round
Spreading dust around the globe
Wings that flutter fast, twinkle, twinkle little star
A fairy to represent everything you see at midnight.

The clock again strikes one o'clock,
I wandered back to my bed and sleep,
I don't know why and I don't know how
Or when I started to wake at midnight.

Chloe Penson (11)
Bishop Perrin School

Habitat

On a log sits a funny frog,
On the mat sleeps a cute cat,
In the trees fly the busy bees,
Underground a badger set has been found,
Through the sky big birds fly,
Between the grass lies an amazing ass,
Under the leaves a happy hedgehog sleeps,
In the river slither, slither,
Exciting animals quiver, quiver.

Emily Dumbrell (11)
Bishop Perrin School

Elephant In The Airport

Elephant in the airport,
Elephant on the runway,
Grabs a jumbo jet
And crashes in the hay.
'Look he's losing his grip.'
'Ouch he's broken my hip.'
Hits the checkout lady
On turns the radio,
I'm Slim Shady.

Joshua Dowden (11)
Bishop Perrin School

Fun Land

F un Land is the best
U p in north west,
N ever expensive, always cheap.

L oads of people have a good time,
A nd enjoy all the wicked rides,
N ow it's time to go pack up the rides and say goodbye,
D addies, children, mothers and toddlers walk away
                                            with tears in their eyes.

Katie-Marie Waygood (10)
Bishop Perrin School

Bomb Site

Under the red-hot rubble,
We could see a big, big bubble,
From a boy who died in a sad, bad war,
The German planes flew down in pain,
When Britain's flew up and gained,
We started to celebrate and rebuild,
When I saw the same school,
All at once I began to cry.

Rebekah Wiltshire (10)
Bishop Perrin School

A Winter's Night

That winter's night,
I cuddled tight,
My mum, my dad, my family.

It was so warm,
It was so cosy,
Sitting near the fire lonely.

I glared out of my little house,
Cuddling my teddy mouse,
Watching the snow blanket the street.

It was so warm,
It was so cosy,
Sitting near the fire lonely.

I opened the door
And the snow covered the floor,
My bare feet freezing cold.

It was so warm,
It was so cosy,
Sitting near the fire lonely.

Charlotte Cleveland (11)
Bishop Perrin School

Candy Land

C andy, candy, candy land,
A lso fun land,
N ever expensive and never cheap,
D o you know where it is?
Y es I do, north, south, west,

L oopy lollies are sold here,
A nd so are other sweets,
N ow it's time to say goodbye,
D o you know who will be here next time?

Hannah Thornley
Bishop Perrin School

The Rage Of The Pied Piper Of Hamlin

'How could this be thy head?
Can't cope,' said he, slamming the
Door in a monstrous way.
He passed the fields, he passed the tree
And then he oathed revenge on thee.

The piper walked, the piper ran,
Until he came to the town again,
He took out his pipe, he played it well,
And all the children were put under his spell,
He led them through the valley,
He led them through the glen
And all of a sudden he ran away
And left them bare with only their skin.

Jacob Modak (10)
Bishop Perrin School

Space

In the middle of space,
There's another type of human race,
They live on Mars,
And don't have cars,
And lie on their backs,
To look at the stars!
If there was a duststorm though,
They'd just throw it like snow!
If they get scared they'll jump down a hole,
And burrow like a mole!

Rhys Wilson (10)
Bishop Perrin School

My Field Of Joy

As the sun rises up
As the shadows appear
My favourite place is getting near
The blossom on the loving trees
The flowers of hope awakening
In the shadow of the field, the trees stand shaking
This field is so special to me
As it's the field of joy, you see.

The birds sing a joyful time
The horses neigh to the disappearing moon
The grass so green a bright delight
With the sun shining all her light
Roses are red as a hero's blood
The moon disappears with the mud
This field is so special to me
As it's the field of joy, you see.

Catherine Hale (11)
Bishop Perrin School

The Slave School

In the slave school, they'll make you work,
If you go you'll go berserk,
If you're insane, you'll get the cane,
Don't be late or you'll meet your fate.

If you fight the teacher's rage,
You'll get locked in a cage,
You'll never fight the teacher's rage,
Because you'll always be locked up in the cage.

Jack Collis
Bishop Perrin School

Undersea Jungle

In an undersea jungle jellyfish roam,
The undersea jungle is a jellyfish home.
In an undersea jungle there's much to see,
If the sharks may come then the divers flee.
Some fish big and some fish small,
Some are short and some are tall.
Fish with different shapes and sizes,
The undersea jungle has big surprises.
There's loads of seaweed everywhere,
You'll come across a catfish lair,
In an undersea jungle, that's what you'll see,
Animal antics for you and me.

Ben Crane (10)
Bishop Perrin School

Imaginary World

I have an imaginary friend
His name is Trotter
And he lives in the land of
Harry Potter.

A swish of the finger,
A zap of a wand,
Hey look over there,
It's the land of
James Bond.

Bang! bang! pop! pop!
Goes his gun
Wait a second
There's Trotter's son.

Adam G Bull (10)
Bishop Perrin School

The Classroom

I touched the gold rusty handle
And the door began to crack,
I walked into the delicate silence
Then terror screamed down my back.

The children sat and stared,
I would have stood and froze,
When I looked around, girls gossiped,
Each boy fiddled with their nose.

I sat down gracefully at the desk
And gage an angelic smile,
'Hi,' I said with a wave of my hand,
I've been waiting to come here for a while.

Soon the class was full of grinning creatures
As I sat down onto my chair,
These grinning creatures kept on grinning,
So I kept on fiddling with my hair.

The lessons flew on throughout the day
And fell into a dreamless dream,
A dream of chocolate or maybe diamonds,
I don't know but I was surely floating in cream.

The dream was soon over, it came to an end,
But I was still half asleep,
A *detention* on my first day of secondary school,
My work was nothing like neat!

Grace McKeown (10)
Bishop Perrin School

Rainbow

If I could hold a colour, I would keep it in my sight,
If I could ride the rainbow, I would hold that feeling tight,
If I could make a rainbow, I would make one every day,
If the rainbow could be my friend, I would laugh and play,
If - such a small word with such a big difference.

Vanessa Hill
Bishop Perrin School

The Haunted House

In the haunted house, no fear lurks at day,
In the haunted house, in a coffin, vampires lay,
If you see a werewolf, it will bite,
If you see a zombie, it is a terrible sight,
If you see a load of bandages, that will be a mummy,
If you see a ghoul, there will be butterflies in your tummy,
In the haunted house, the butler will be your host,
Your host will run away if he sees a ghost.

Manoj Athukorala (11)
Bishop Perrin School

Animals

If I saw a bear, it would sit, stand and stare,
If I saw a rat, I would run for my cat,
If I saw a snake, I would kill it with a rake,
If I saw a bird, I would think I was a nerd,
If I saw a spider, I would drink a lot of cider,
It is so tiny, yet it makes things so shiny.

Rahil Davda (11)
Bishop Perrin School

The Bombing Of Britain

Hitler and his men
Filled up the sky with bombers
Tried to get the throne
Londoner's were terrified,
Tried to destroy our nation.

Brandon Robinson (11)
Crane Park Primary School

Why War . . . Here And Now?

Why are bombs dropping from the sky?
Why does Hitler want to kill?
It is no sweet pie,
It is giving us the chills!

As Hitler disturbs our lives,
He has put our lives at risk!
As our hearts are being pulled out with knives,
It is no longer a risk!

Why does Hitler want to disturb,
The only people unknown?
The bombs in the night are hitting the curb,
They did not even have a loan!

Hitler will send no warning,
So beware of the danger ahead!
There will be no time for laundering,
That was what Hitler had said!

So slowly we are dying,
So quickly we are dying!
We don't know where to hide,
Because Hitler had no pride!

Harjit Padda (11)
Crane Park Primary School

Devastating Bombs

The street is pitch-dark,
The sky lit up like fireworks,
Terror everywhere.

Jasvinder Singh (10)
Crane Park Primary School

Destruction Of Britain

Quick, quick, fire, fire,
Flames rise higher and higher,
Sirens wailing louder and louder,
Helter-skelter to the shelter,
Bombs dropping nearer and nearer,
Things become quiet and people are dearer.

Michael Paul Rosato (10)
Crane Park Primary School

World War II

Germans bomb our homes,
Our precious city falls down,
Families are split up.

People being killed,
Germans bomb London all over,
Shelters being filled
People fleeing for their lives,
English soldiers miss their wives.

Josh Kearney (10)
Crane Park Primary School

Destruction

Families are split,
Germany bombed our precious city,
Soldiers died fighting,
It is the Second World War.
It was really terrible.

Brendan Stanbridge (11)
Crane Park Primary School

Witness Of War

Crash, bang, crackle the sound invading your ears,
German's flying everywhere,
Children being evacuated, parents in lots of tears,
Not enough coupons even for a chair.

Soldiers trained to be very alert.
Everyone in Britain full of melancholy.
Government getting everyone to knit just one shirt,
Because there wasn't enough clothing to fit a 30cm dolly.

The Blitz killing people cold-blooded,
Not just the British but Germans too.
It's worse than the whole world being flooded,
Doesn't help if you've got the flu.

I now hope you know what it's like,
You're so lucky to have food, clothes and even a bike.

Ashley Martins (10)
Crane Park Primary School

World War

The blackout made it easier to snooze!
Armies couldn't see our homes,
We think that Hitler will lose, but we still moan!
Hitler is bad,
Hitler is greedy,
We all think he's mad to take over England,
We will close in on Hitler's army at speed,
It is a nice blue sky,
Over men in combat,
We do not know why Hitler is bad!
We do not know where he's at?
He wore a hat
And that's that!

Michael Pereira (10)
Crane Park Primary School

Distraught Families

World War II was a huge nightmare
Many people were dying
Incendiary bombs dropping through the air
Life is complicated but we keep on trying.

Victory is hard to achieve
Because the war is severe
Evacuees had to pack up and leave
Most poor children didn't even shed a tear.

Losing your family makes you so depressed
Especially if you're being adopted
Living new lives makes you distressed
But it's for the best even if you feel besotted.

Everyone tried to survive the war
And tried to stop Hitler from killing anymore.

Rochelle Green (10)
Crane Park Primary School

The War Years

World War Two was terrifying
There were air-raid shelters
The people were heart-broken
There were loads of helpers
Bombs were falling
Everyone was storming
Everything was appalling
Some people drooling
There was a loud siren
People were screaming
There were firemen
People were helping
People were rebuilding
Everyone was helping.

Jade Hammett (10)
Crane Park Primary School

Bombs, Bombs And More Bombs

Hitler started the war,
Trying to rule over us,
But now he's becoming a bore,
Causing nothing but a fuss.

Rationing started in '39,
He stopped us having proper food,
Before the war it was fine,
He is being really rude.

During the night,
When the siren sounds,
We have to take flight,
To hide under those mounds.

The war is nearly over,
So we won't have to take cover.

Samantha Bragg (11)
Crane Park Primary School

World War II

Hitler the heartless is marauding London
People are begging for their lives
Families all over are being undone
This all happens when war arrives.

Bombs are falling like rain
The sky is full of smoke,
People are running away
I can't help but choke.

As people are dying and crying,
I know that I have to help,
People there lying
As I know that Jesus was there to help.

Eric Osei Tutu (10)
Crane Park Primary School

Upsurge Of Hell

Valorous warriors drive in their mechanisation
Whilst taken further away from civilisation
Their fighting brave, but still, they're nervous,
Little children are living luxurious.

Squadrons and squadrons die,
Whilst little children eat pie,
Germans scuttle from the scene,
Whilst non-evacuees don't know where they've been.

Boats are torpedoed,
Whilst T-shirts are sewn,
Traitors are given exile
And forced to sleep on a ragged pile.

Lands have been carelessly crossed,
Little children are bossed.

Georgia-May Cooper (11)
Crane Park Primary School

Cascading Bombs

Whirling bombs hit us,
Cabash, cabang,
One day it hit a bus
And the blaring siren rang.

I look and frown, dissatisfied,
I know that God is our ally,
So please help me to hide,
I know that I might die.

In Heaven I know it's a wonderful place,
But down here it's erratic,
Germany is destroying England's human race,
I can't help but think the Germans are being dramatic.

Now the war has nearly ended,
I have to go and get things mended.

Kiana Jade Rhianna Smith (10)
Crane Park Primary School

The Battle Of Hell

The battle has begun,
Hell has broken lose,
All the children are sad,
At Christmas I didn't have any goose.

I was stabbed in the arm,
And my friend got shot and died,
My child got sent to the farm
And the children in London cried.

All day and night the bombs go down,
I hate my life,
All bombs go down in town,
All the children around me have headlice.

Most of the men had to work in the mine,
My life is almost running out of time.

Ella May Gibson (10)
Crane Park Primary School

World War II Poem

I'm scared and young,
I have no home to live,
Every time the bomb falls I twist my tongue,
All the things I give.

I hope the war will end,
The children clinging to their kin,
Will horror be erratic or around the bend,
It seems to me war is a sin.

The soldiers trudging on the slimy mud,
The valorous people fighting back,
The ground is splattered with blood,
Of men forced to attack.

This terrible, tragic war,
How can the people stand anymore?

Shivani Patel (11)
Crane Park Primary School

World War II

The war has begun, Germans are terrorising the place,
The violating, devastating Germans we hate,
Bombs, guns blasting in our face.

The notorious Germans using us as bait,
We found a unique shelter, better than the rest,
The Germans are coming, hide.

People dying is not the best,
The Germans are now denying,
Evacuees leaving home.

Some children have lice,
Some need to comb,
Many mothers are nice,
I quickly count to eleven,
And wish *God* to take me to Heaven.

Shahnaz Islam (11)
Crane Park Primary School

Eternal War

I walk down the street,
As windows glare at me.
There's a poignant sting on my feet!
But what else can I see?
People killing, people dying!
I hate this chronic and severe sight!
People mournful, people sighing!
Oh God, take me above to the light.
We amble cautiously, looking for shelter!
As deafening bombs drop by,
I pray rapidly and I feel much better . . .
But then I fall on my knees and cry!
A brisk breeze runs through my face,
I notice I no longer exist in this place . . .

Nilofar Afzali (10)
Crane Park Primary School

World War II

The prayers come down,
Everyone on their knees,
They are edged with a frown,
And they all beg . . . 'Please, please, please.'

The men are ready to fight,
But nervous too,
The women are in a fright,
The children don't know what to do!

The bombs come down continuously,
As the buildings blow up, what a mess,
The Germans come slowly,
When we now have less.

This is all like one big bend,
So this must be the end.

Yousof Yosofzai (10)
Crane Park Primary School

Savage War

What is this war about?
I detest this war.
There are so many shouts,
What is it for?

All the bullets soaring past me,
All the bombs s w o o p i n g towards me.
Where is the enemy? I can't see,
This war is evil - killing a helpless bee.

Why do we have to do this?
Hitler is so *gloomy* and *sinful*.
All I really want is a mother's kiss,
Did Hitler need to be so voracious and dreadful?

Oh, I do loathe this war so much,
Hitler is so supreme; all he needs to do to kill is touch.

Hamed Alemzada (10)
Crane Park Primary School

War Devastation

I look out of the window at the devastation
Of London cities
Which have been destroyed, every creation
Now everyone alive has their pities
So would my mum if she was alive.
Even Daddy has gone to fight in the war
I am surprised, how did I survive?
I wish there was no more
As each bomb falls
It breaks the heart
Of an owner of the old few walls
Which are now broken, all fallen apart.
I sit on my own
For when I went to the shop I came back and had no home.

Chanel Downes (11)
Crane Park Primary School

Silent Death

Now we're at war with Germany,
My mum and dad are dead,
It's not fair to me,
All these thoughts going through my head.

There's an air raid going on right now,
Over the top of my house.
'Ouch!' Now I'm trapped, how I'll get out I don't know how,
Over in the corner there's a squashed mouse.

Now I can't help my eyes from closing,
If I'm dying at least I'm safe,
Well, now I hate the Germans, I hope they'll end up losing!
Now I can't even feel my face,
I hope Ginger's going to be OK, that's my little kitten,
Go on now, you can win the war Great Britain!

Jade Rayner-Jones (10)
Crane Park Primary School

Help!

The life has gone away,
To the destructive life of Germany,
They only want us to pay,
I want it to *stop* but they won't listen to me.

Please stop Germany from dominating us,
It is not fair, they've got us trapped.
God, please, we should surrender. We must,
My family are dead. I should be perhaps!

The bombs are coming, all are running,
As they shout, they spit and shoot.
Some Germans like it, though, for the money,
But all the children are so cute.

> But now is my time to go and die,
> So goodbye.

Chloe Shaw (10)
Crane Park Primary School

The War Has Just Begun

The war has just begun, bombs screaming
To land in the centre of the Earth.
The children were crying and their tears glimmering,
Men marched and said, 'Get off our turf!'
Hitler commanding to fight,
And the boats sank,
And the men had a fright,
Men fought with a tank,
Lots of people were dying,
Everyone was worried,
Mums were crying,
Army men hurried,
The river was polluted,
The king was saluted.

Callum Creighton (10)
Crane Park Primary School

World War II Poem

Children travelling on trains,
Going to the countryside,
Playing games in the rain,
Not enjoying the ride.

Arriving at the countryside trying to make new friends,
While wishing they were back home with Mum and Dad,
Hoping the war soon ends,
While keeping notes in my new pad.

The countryside is nice and clean,
There's always something boring too,
All the nasty things they make me do is keeping me lean,
They are always telling me what to do.

I want my mum and dad right here,
But for now I'll just shed one tear.

Emma O'Brien (10)
Crane Park Primary School

World War II

What a war - inhumane, death, blood.
The guns and bombs rattle.
Towards the front the soldiers flood,
Marching to battle.

Are the soldiers ready to fight?
But scared too.
All the children are worried tonight,
But what shall we do?

Everyone wanted to appear.
Thousands and thousands of people were dying
And there were many tears,
People were crying.

Their country they must defend.
Will this be the end?

Kiran Singh (10)
Crane Park Primary School

Deafening Cacophony

The war has started
There was explosions
It caused danger
Children were crying
Families were devastated
War ended, lives were safer.

Kuljit Padda (11)
Crane Park Primary School

Wishes

W itches, elves and fairies,
I like fairy tales,
S tories are made up,
H uge giants,
E veryone likes the princess,
S trong and handsome princes.

Aasia Najumi (7)
Dormers Wells Junior School

Prince

P owerful and strong,
R escues princesses,
I think he is a hero,
N ice, handsome and
C lever.
E veryone loves the prince.

Simran Juttla (8)
Dormers Wells Junior School

Giants

G iants are bad.
I hate giants,
A lways angry and mad,
N ever kind or good,
T hey are huge, hairy and nasty.

Shaun Rockall (8)
Dormers Wells Junior School

Witch

W icked, evil and nasty,
I n the sky she flies,
T ricks and spells she makes
C ackling and laughing,
H er hat is black and pointed.

Ikram Musse (7)
Dormers Wells Junior School

Beast

B ig and ugly,
E vil and bad,
A ngry and nasty,
S trong and powerful,
T errifying and frightening.

Vickram Singh (8)
Dormers Wells Junior School

Star

S hiny, sparkly and bright,
T winkles through the night,
A ll stars are glittery,
R eally sharp and light.

Ali Abbas (7)
Dormers Wells Junior School

The Writer Of This Poem
(Based on 'The Writer Of This Poem' by Roger McGough)

The writer of this poem is
As white as Gandalf,
As clever as a geek,
As sweet as Miss Honey,
As noisy as children.

As hot as coffee,
As high as a mountain,
As brave as an astronaut,
As thin as a pencil.

As pretty as dancers,
As magical as Gandalf,
As black as a knight,
As bright as sunshine.

As pink as a pig,
As sharp as a needle,
As fun as literacy,
As shiny as gold.

Shiala Suleman (8)
Dormers Wells Junior School

The Writer Of This Poem
(Based on 'The Writer Of This Poem' by Roger McGough)

The writer of this poem is
As smart as a calculator,
As fast as a rabbit,
As strong as a terminator.

As sharp as spikes,
As shiny as a crown,
As small as a mouse,
As funny as a clown.

Dwayne Boyce (8)
Dormers Wells Junior School

The Writer Of This Poem
(Based on 'The Writer Of This Poem' by Roger McGough)

The writer of this poem is
As swift as Shadowfax,
As wise as Sauron,
As tall as Treebeard,
As skilled as Legolas.

As brave as an astronaut,
As clever as termites,
As magical as Saraman,
As tricky as Aragorn.

As colourful as a rainbow,
As sharp as nails,
As thin as paper,
As strong as a castle.

As runny as water,
As slippery as ice,
As hot as a blaze.

Amardeep Dosanjh (8)
Dormers Wells Junior School

Racism

R acism can come in jokes and games
A nd lots of people get murdered because of it
C rime investigators don't do much about it
I t is racism that brings us to war.
S ome people even commit suicide because they
                              cannot take the abuse
M any people might disagree with me, but I don't
                        care, I will stand by my opinion.

Akash Gurung (10)
Dormers Wells Junior School

Bullying

You take mine and my friend's money,
You're so wrong, you think it's funny.
You are big and naughty,
You need to find maturity.
You could be as sweet as honey.

You poke people with your ruler,
You think bullying will make you cooler,
You give me loads of deep cuts,
I feel like hiding in the teachers' huts.

Then, after the cuts comes the blood,
When you cover me with mud.
This might have turned into a game of 'Had',
But good always beats the bad.

Humaira Aslam (9)
Dormers Wells Junior School

The Writer Of This Poem
(Based on 'The Writer Of This Poem' by Roger McGough)

The writer of this poem is
Smaller than a house,
As clever as a doctor,
As quiet as a mouse.

As handsome as a prince,
As fast as a hare,
As spooky as a monster,
As scary as a bear.

As cheeky as a monkey,
As thin as a pencil,
As strong as a lion,
As lovely as a stencil.

Abdurahman Mohammed (8)
Dormers Wells Junior School

The Writer Of This Poem
(Based on 'The Writer Of This Poem' by Roger McGough)

The writer of this poem is
As bright as the sunshine,
As smooth as fur
As thin as a line.

As sweet as honey,
As smart as a hare,
As pretty as a flower
Who always takes care.

As happy as a clown,
As kind as a nurse,
As lucky as a fairy,
As clever as verse.

Anesu Madamombe (9)
Dormers Wells Junior School

The Writer Of This Poem
(Based on 'The Writer Of This Poem' by Roger McGough)

The writer of this poem is
As strong as a gorilla,
As small as an ant,
As gentle as a gentleman.

As fast as a cheetah,
As slow as a tortoise,
As happy as a clown,
As silly as a bully.

As good as a vitamin,
As quiet as a library,
As busy as a butler,
As bright as gold.

Mohamed Omar (9)
Dormers Wells Junior School

The Writer Of This Poem
(Based on 'The Writer Of This Poem' by Roger McGough)

The writer of this poem is
Steven Gangadeen.
As strong as a whale,
As gentle as a mouse,
As fast as a cheetah.

As slow as a snail,
As happy as a ladybird,
As silly as a child,
As scary as a shark.

As small as a rabbit,
As fit as a wrestler,
As scary as an alien.

Steven Gangadeen (8)
Dormers Wells Junior School

The Writer Of This Poem
(Based on 'The Writer Of This Poem' by Roger McGough)

The writer of this poem is
As pretty as a princess,
As strong as an acrobat,
As gentle as soft skin.

As fast as a hare,
As slow as a slug,
As happy as a lark,
As silly as a mule.

As quick as a flick,
As sly as a fox,
As cheeky as a monkey,
As cute as a dolphin.

Sara Haider (9)
Dormers Wells Junior School

The Writer Of This Poem
(Based on 'The Writer Of This Poem' by Roger McGough)

The writer of this poem is
As beautiful as a rose,
As strong as a body builder.

As gentle as a butterfly,
As fast as a cheetah,
As slow as a tortoise,
As happy as a pop star,
As silly as a clown.

As bright as a sun,
As quiet as a library,
As good as a diamond,
As busy as an airport.

Maham Qureshi (9)
Dormers Wells Junior School

The Writer Of This Poem
(Based on 'The Writer Of This Poem' by Roger McGough)

The writer of this poem is
As tall as a tower,
As strong as a wrestler.

As gentle as a baby,
As fast as a hare,
As slow as a tortoise,
As happy as a sun,
As silly as a monkey.

As quiet as a library,
As tiny as an ant,
As soft as wool,
As white as snow.

Femisha Patel (8)
Dormers Wells Junior School

Racism

R acism is as terrible as war!
A t times you may get angry, sad or more.
C alling people names, hurting their feelings!
I t can take a long time healing.
S ometimes people get violent!
M any people suffer and are silent.

Saminder Brar & Sanjay Mall (10)
Dormers Wells Junior School

Racism

R acism is horrible, hateful and hurtful
A ttacking occurs after racism
C an it stop?
I f someone is racist tell somebody
S ometimes racism turns into violence
M any people have suffered racism in silence.

Shanka Fernando & Daman Johal (11)
Dormers Wells Junior School

My Big Sister

Chocolate-snatcher
Boy-catcher
Hand-smacker
Work-slacker
Big-scarer
Sneaky-darer
Room-mucker
Toy-chucker
Story-seller
Secret-teller.

Sophie Pearson (10)
Echelford Primary School

Elephant

An elephant is a massive bulldozer, always on the move.
Ground-rattler.
Its ears are giant paper plates coloured in grey,
Its legs are giant pillars, hard and thick.
Its skin is jagged, rough sandpaper.
Its trunk is a snorkel and a wriggling snake.
Elephants are never-forgetting machines, so be careful.
Mice tramplers.
Its eyes are blocks of everlasting memory,
Its tail is a flexible paintbrush,
Its body is a firm brick wall,
Its tusks are ivory jewellery.

Sheena Petrovini (11)
Echelford Primary School

Sharks

A shark is an eating machine,
A shark is a ferocious beast,
It can bite through a whale carcass,
Sharks are incredible eaters, they eat non-stop,
A shark's body is as strong as steel,
Sharks are sleepless animals through night and day,
When a shark's tooth falls out it grows another one,
Sharks are vicious,
Sharks are not mammals,
They have ferocious jaws,
Their bodies are built like tanks.

Russell Ashwood (11)
Echelford Primary School

Sharks

A shark is an eating machine,
He darts through the water without any sleep.
A life destroyer,
A speedy killer, 24 hours a day.
Ready for anything when ready to attack.
Eyes of wisdom,
Teeth are machetes,
Energy is eternal!
He crashes through waves at 100mph,
Skin is as smooth as silk,
The shark has an armoured body
    which is impossible to scratch.

David Merchant (11)
Echelford Primary School

Elephants

An elephant's tail is an endless . . .
Swinging rope.

Its belly is a hot-air balloon
Tied to the Earth by a tail and trunk.

Its ears are fans that cool you down.

Its legs are hairy coconut trees.

An elephant's eyes are large stepping-stones.

Its skin is a long, dusty, dirt track.

An elephant is not a friend for life . . .

Leah Bulley (11)
Echelford Primary School

Air Raid

Bombs are now falling,
People are crawling,
Down, underground,
That's where they're bound.

Bombs are exploding!
Buildings which were eroding
Are crumbling with a crash,
And factories are smashed.

Bombs have stopped falling,
People are crawling,
Up above ground,
That's where they're bound.

Bombs aren't exploding,
Some buildings are still eroding.
They aren't crumbling with a crash
And factories aren't being smashed.

London is smouldering,
London's still standing,
Its people are bold,
Their hope is not cold.

Adam Huse (11)
Echelford Primary School

Rhino

A rhino's body is an armoured tank,
Its horn is a sharp sword,
Its legs are thick steel poles.
When it runs, it sounds like a roaring train,
A rampaging beast,
A fearless hunter,
It can break every bone in your body.

Andrew Salt (11)
Echelford Primary School

Animals

A cup of sharks,
A mouth of crocodiles,
A bin of cockroaches,
A hand of elephants.

A belly of dolphins,
A flutter of sharks,
A cuddle of cockroaches,
A home of slugs.

A bald patch of hair,
A bath of crocodiles,
A rustle of cats,
A barrel of slugs.

Jamie Cork (10)
Echelford Primary School

Elephant

An elephant's body is a charging gigantic tank,
An earth-shaker as it stomps through the country,
Food-taker from other animals,
Slow walker,
Its ears are huge china plates,
Its skin is rough sandpaper,
A memory machine,
The trunk is a long, thick, swinging rope,
Tusks are sharp daggers,
Its eyes are bright, staring buttons in the night.

Lora Thomas (11)
Echelford Primary School

My Best Things

Coke from the fridge, oranges and pears,
My dad when he does all of his shares.
Spending money on ice cream and jelly,
Watching cartoons on my favourite telly.
Going away on an aeroplane,
Playing with my PlayStation 2 games.
End of days, weeks and especially terms,
Do what we want but take it in turns.
Going swimming with my cousins and friends,
Buying them all a pack of pens.
Eating all of my favourite dinner,
Finishing first and being a winner!

Kelly Woods (11)
Echelford Primary School

What Is A Dragon?

A dragon is a red and orange
burning ball of fire.

It is a powerful,
leathery green tree.

It is an enormous,
horrid, smelly beast.

It is a huge beady eye,
watching me wherever I go.

It is the boiling sun
high up in the sky.

Hannah Wakeman (11)
Echelford Primary School

A To Z Poem

A attempted to act happily in class.
B bounced in joy at A.
C called A a rubbish actor.
D disturbed everyone.
E elbowed his teacher.
F failed in a test.
G got told off.
H hit harry.
I improved on his work.
J jumped off a desk.
K kicked Kevin.
L lied about liking literacy.
M marched around the classroom.
N napped in the classroom.
O opened his teacher's drawer.
P picked on Paul.
Q queued to get his work marked.
R ripped Robert's work up.
S ss'ed at Steve.
T took Robert's ripped up work.
U underlined his wrong work.
V visited the headmaster.
W waited for Wendy.
X X-rayed one of the x-men.
Y yelled at one of the other teachers.
Z zoomed around the classroom.

Georgia Grant (10)
Echelford Primary School

What Is A Dragon?

A dragon's scales are green slippers,
A dragon is a glass tank with claws,
A dragon's breath is a yellow and orange
                      sauce on ice cream.

Chelby Meade (10)
Echelford Primary School

Kennings Sea

Shark-swarmer
Wave-roarer.

Shell-collector
Water-floater.

Fish-catcher,
Catfish-scratcher.

Boat-drifter
A little fisher.

Georgia Page (10)
Echelford Primary School

The Ox

The ox is as big as a cow and a bull,
Its horns are like long swords,
Eyeballs as sharp as bombs,
His body is like a bundle of dynamite,
An ox is like two bulls.
Unto him a child is like
A pair of twigs with leafy hair -
A portion of gravel!

Tom Dunbar (8)
Echelford Primary School

What Is A Dragon?

A dragon is a leathery Cheesestring,
A dragon is a ferocious beast,
A dragon is an old sack,
A dragon is a smoky, drooling lizard,
A dragon is a squirming baby,
A dragon is a rubbery terrorist!

Fay Yeoman (11)
Echelford Primary School

Road Rage

Rally-racer
Petrol-waster
Horn-beeper
Petrol-eater
Road-racer
Turbo-racer
Legible-learner
Easy-turner.

Greg Giles (11)
Echelford Primary School

My Cheetah

My cheetah is a gazelle destroyer,
His spots are balls of fire galloping through the air,
He effortlessly sprints at 65mph.

His tail is an endless grey elephant's trunk,
Teeth are sharp daggers in battle,
Back legs are jet-propelled,
Eyes are red like the blood gushing from a gazelle body.
Fastest animal on Earth, run, run, run . . .

Michael Adamson (10)
Echelford Primary School

What Is A Ghost?

A ghost is an evil part of air,
It is an ear-piercing, screaming, rotting spirit,
It is a sobbing child whose mum has left,
It is a menacing old man,
It is an angry person from another dimension
                            full of vengeance.

David Gudge (10)
Echelford Primary School

Mums!

House-shouter
Big-hitter
Champion-moaner
Queen-phoner
Eyeshadow mad
Rapid-cleaner
They're scared of spiders
But not good hiders.

Stuart Donald (10)
Echelford Primary School

The Giraffe

How tiny is a child to a giraffe's eye?
Hair like a brown leaf
Shining through the air.
A head like a mushroom
Down in the ground.
Arms like sticks
From the big bushy tree.

Jack Cooper (8)
Echelford Primary School

What Is A Ghost?

A ghost is a cold mist,
It is a soft, fluffy cloud.
A ghost is a screaming sheet,
It is a quick spinning fan,
It's a deafening white pencil,
It's a long, spooky, misty shirt.

Zoe Stanton (10)
Echelford Primary School

Demon The Forest Fox

Demon sneaks around from side to side,
He does not care about his pride.
He scavenges for his dinner,
But never is a winner.
He runs around all of the night,
He never sees sunny light.

Demon's ginger fur is soft like silk,
The only thing he drinks is snowy white milk.
He wears a black velvety cloak,
And sails in a mini brown boat.
When Demon is seen he gives a loud yelp,
When people are around they shout for help.

Lucy Thurlow (10)
Echelford Primary School

Worst Things

I hate cauliflower and smelly fish,
Putting Brussels in my dish.

Annoying people like boys,
Showing off with their Game Boys.

I hate being ill,
Waiting an hour to get to the till.

Fighting with friends,
Falling off my bike, riding around bends.

I hate some perfumes
Being sprayed in the bedroom.

I hate slimy frogs,
Being bitten by cats or dogs.

Christina Cope (11)
Echelford Primary School

My Mum

She's a good cooker,
A cool looker.
She's a super shouter,
A money counter.
She's a make-up addictor,
A friend called Victor.
She's a car driver,
A late arriver.
She's a child lover,
A champion mother.

Maria Stanton (10)
Echelford Primary School

What Am I?

My eyes are the green, green grass.
My eyes are the daggers that see.

My fangs are the needles that puncture,
My fangs are the poisonous enemy.

My body is a slimy piece of spaghetti,
My body is a slippery, soft soap.

What am I?

Answer: A snake!

Sian Louise Thomas (10)
Echelford Primary School

What Is A Dragon?

A dragon is a peppery, hissing orange fireball.
It is an olive-green, scaly snake.
Its breath is like pungent, putrid cabbage,
It is a roaring, growling alligator.

Ben Skilling (10)
Echelford Primary School

Wicked Weasel

Wicked Weasel creeps round the house,
His soft padded paws, quiet as a mouse.
Stealing food from the larder,
Finding him is even harder!
Slithering through pipes like a snake,
It sounds like a ghost if you are awake!

His fiendish face, his wicked smile,
None of his paw prints are on police file!
He has brown scruffy fur like a tramp,
Wherever he goes he leaves his own stamp.
With a lash of his tail and a print of his paw,
He leaves his mark when he breaks the law.

If he gets caught he will fail,
And spend the rest of his life in jail.
If he dies there will be no tears,
All you'll hear are whoops and cheers!
So if you are in town one day, please note,
That if you meet this weasel fiend, be sure that you can cope!

Chloe Clark (10)
Echelford Primary School

Dogs

Dogs are fierce dragons guarding their owners,
Their big, brown, beautiful eyes are full of wisdom.
They devour their bones with their machete-like teeth.
They are shoe wreckers.
Dogs are cat-slaughter machines
And home destroyers.
Their energy rate is an eternal treadmill.
They are non-stop feeders.
They sleep eternally as a bear would through winter.

Liam O'Shea (11)
Echelford Primary School

An Elephant

An elephant's leg is a trunk from a tree,
A harmless plant-eating giant.
Its ears are massive fans,
Moving back and forwards in the heat of the day.
Its a loader, carrying logs from the forest.
A loud noisy speaker.
An elephant's body is a hard rock.
A long-living animal.
Its trunk is as long as a snake.
An elephant's tail is like a rope that swings,
Its tusks are like two swords ready to fight.
A rampaging animal
But it's scared of mice!

Shyam Petrovini (11)
Echelford Primary School

Killer Whales

Whales are plankton devourers,
Swimming, they spend hour after hour.
They are fast thinkers,
They are not stinkers!
They're the acrobats of the big blue sea,
They're much, much faster than you or me will ever be.
Black and white,
They are the killers of the sea.
By day they play,
By night they fight.
Whales are my favourite animals,
Guess what, they're even mammals.

Andrew Trott (11)
Echelford Primary School

Magic Box
(Based on 'Magic Box' by Kit Wright)

I will put in my box . . .

The smell of my mum's magnificent washing!
The fluffy, furry fur of a plodding panda!
Tickets to hot, hot happy Hollywood.

I will put in my box . . .

The sight of a horse galloping in the air!
Drinking a glorious glass of fresh water!
Seeing a dancing dotty dolphin swimming in the water!

I will put in my box . . .

The smell of a roast dinner lying in my tummy!
The fluffiest, furriest teddies in the whole world!
The terrifying taste of Chinese and Indian food!

My box is made from the purplest admirable, amazing amethyst.
My box is decorated with the daintiest diamonds in the whole world.
My box is held together by perfect platinum.
I shall ski in my box until it's just a little stone.

Bridie Smithers (9)
Echelford Primary School

Have You Ever Heard Of It?

A crackle of crocodiles,
A rustle of rats,
A mouthful of mice,
A slimeful of slugs,
A pair of pears.

A whisper of lions,
A cough of cockroaches,
An eggful of elephants,
A snap of sharks,
A hairful of snakes.

Jessie Beetham (11)
Echelford Primary School

My Magic Box
(Based on 'Magic Box' by Kit Wright)

I will put in my box . . .

A tiger tiggling, tigglish toes,
Fabulous, friendly and famous people to meet ever day
And the first laugh floating freely and friendly around the room
from my sister.

I will put in my box . . .

The ability to live under the clear blue sea,
To click my fingers and have whatever I desire,
And to fly freely around the big open sky
And fly in and out of the clouds.

My box is decorated by . . .

The shiniest diamond in the whole wide world.

My box is made of . . .

Ebony, the most expensive wood in the whole wide world.

In my box I shall . . .

Sunbathe in the hottest country there ever was
And I shall ride the fastest horse in the whole wide world
Wherever I desire!

Lauren Meadows (9)
Echelford Primary School

Jonny Wilkinson

Shirt-swapper,
Goal-stopper,
Ball-hogger,
Quick-jogger,
Ball-catcher,
Kick-snatcher,
Hard-kicker,
Penalty-taker,
Cup-winner!

Glenn Olding (11)
Echelford Primary School

Alphabet Poem

A acted in the school play,
B batted E's apple,
C caught A in a game,
D dipped C in a bin,
E entered the hockey team
F fought a fight against X,
G got goosebumps,
H held a hot-dog,
I iced a cake,
J juggled with a pen,
K kicked the football,
L licked J's ice lolly,
M munched the teacher's Mars Bar,
N nudged P,
O opened the book,
P pinched Q's writing pen,
Q qualified in the final of the hockey team,
R refused to do his science,
S slid out of school,
T turned off the tap,
U used L to get his football from the tree,
V vanished when the test started,
W watched Lara Croft 2,
X X-rayed himself,
Y yawned in the 2 hour maths lesson,
Z zoomed through his work.

Luke Rogers (9)
Echelford Primary School

The Magic Box
(Based on 'Magic Box' by Kit Wright)

I will put in my box . . .

A lovely bar of chocolate
A wholesome house made of sweets and sour liquorice laces
A mysterious baby monkey sitting on my lap.

I will put in my box . . .

The first smile of a baby
The smell of roast dinner when it's cooking
The first word of a baby.

I will put in my box . . .

The sun and sparkling stars
A tip of a tongue touching the fire
The softest singing voice of an angel.

I will put in my box . . .

The white snowflakes that look so sparkly
The clear blue sky
The sound of the blue sparkling sea.

My box is made out of . . .

Real gold, decorated with diamonds.
I shall live in my box and treasure all the things inside it.

Samantha Bromley (9)
Echelford Primary School

What Is A Dragon?

A dragon is a demolishing, fire-breathing red neck.
A dragon is a leathery, smoky fire bird.
A dragon is a smelly, roaring demon.
A dragon's mouth is a red-hot furnace.
A dragon is a stomping, rubber giant.
A dragon is a winter-hiding lizard.

Samuel Tucker (10) & Ben Paget (11)
Echelford Primary School

Alphabet Poem

A attacked the teacher with a pen
B bit into the teacher's arm,
C camped in a tent on the school field,
D demolished the classroom,
E electrocuted everyone in the classroom,
F flew across the classroom,
G gave all his school books away,
H hit the teacher on the head,
I was irritating D in the classroom,
J jumped around the classroom,
K kicked S and S cried,
L licked the teacher's lolly,
M moaned at the teacher,
N nudged M then fell into A then fell into C,
O organised a fight in the playground,
P played in the classroom,
Q queued up in the school toilets,
R ruled the whole school,
S sighed at the teacher,
T told a lie about A,
U used a pencil to poke A in the eye,
V visited the headmaster's office,
W whistled in the classroom,
X X-rayed P,
Y yawned in class,
Z zoomed out of the classroom.

Melissa Soden (9)
Echelford Primary School

Kennings Sea

Wave-smasher
    Beach-crasher
Children's pleasure
    Human-leisure
Man-killer.

David Amaddio (11)
Echelford Primary School

My Magic Box
(Based on 'Magic Box' by Kit Wright)

I will put in the box . . .

A rumbling, rude, rabid, ruling rhinoceros running round the rocks.
A platypus peeking from under the water.
An anaconda ambushing areas of the swamp.

I will put in the box . . .

The ability to fly in the sky.
A python purring, prickly in the mud.
A shark shining in the deep blue sea.

I will put in my box . . .

A cheesy slice of Italian pizza.
A cornet of my favourite ice cream
And the delicate taste of Walker's crisps.

I will put in my box . . .

A tasty tender turkey turned down my throat.
A crunchy chicken in my belly.
The tip of a turnip touching my tooth.

My box is made of . . .

Some magic mahogany
Held together with legs of tarantulas
And studded with platinum.

I will put in my box . . .

Snowboarding down Everest.
Jumping in the sea
And flying over the clouds.

Joseph Swabey (9)
Echelford Primary School

Learning Your ABC

A attempted to cover the room in paint.
B broke F's pencil.
C covered D with paper.
D dodged detention.
E elbowed B.
F fell in the pool.
G graffited his book.
H hung on the teacher's door.
I injured himself by jumping off his desk.
J jumped off the wall bars.
K kicked J's chair.
L licked Q's lolly.
M munched N's crisps.
N nicked M's homework.
O organised a swimming pool for the school.
P pinched M's arm.
Q queued up for lunch at 10 o'clock.
R ran into the art room.
S slipped into the art room.
T tried to rob the school.
U used all the paint.
V vandalised the headmaster's room.
W won the race.
X executed the teachers.
Y yelled at the teacher.
Z zoomed around the classroom.

Josh Guidera (10)
Echelford Primary School

My Magic Box
(Based on 'Magic Box' by Kit Wright)

I will put in my box . . .
the perfect slice of pineapple, pepperoni, pepper pizza that I will enjoy,
the taste of chocolate melting in my mouth,
a cheeky monkey sitting on a tree, munching bananas.

I will put in my box . . .
the ability to fly like a bird,
a blue relaxing bubbled bath.

I will put in my box . . .
the sound of the waves crashing as I walk along the beach,
the New York mall where I will go and shop till I drop.

My box is made out of gold and silver decorated
with dazzling diamonds and glittering gems.
I shall live in my box and treasure it forever.

Hannah McDonough (10)
Echelford Primary School

Who Helped The Rats?

Who gave the rats McDonald's?
Who fed those filthy rats?
Who gave them water to drink?
Who gave them good habitats?

Who gave the rats burgers?
Who wants to feed those rats?
Who gave them juice to drink?
Why are they bigger than bats?

Who gave the rats chips?
Why feed those stinky rats?
Who gave them cola to drink?
Why they're as big as hats!

Charles Whitley (9)
Echelford Primary School

Magic Box
(Based on 'Magic Box' by Kit Wright)

I will put in the box . . .
The dancing droplets of a divine dolphin
diving into the depths of the deep blue sea.
The softness of a stripy tiger
slipping silently through the sun-crisped grass.
The silky touch of a lion's lovely, long, locked mane.

I will put in the box . . .
The ability to live underwater
floating through the green seaweed like a tropical fish.
To fly through the air like a bird swooping round the clouds.
To stay and play with a pack of beautiful bottlenose dolphins.

My box is made of . . .
Silver silk and glittery gold.
It's decorated with rectangular, red rubies,
perfect peridots and enchanting emeralds.
It's held together by spiky stars.

I will play with dolphins in my box.
I will dance on the waves of the Mediterranean Sea in my box.
I will live in a place where people and animals
don't get hurt - in my box.

Emma Burrows (9)
Echelford Primary School

Best Things

Playing football
that's really cool.

Roast beef my favourite dinner
Mum's slices getting thinner!

The television gives me frights
and I like lots of late nights.

I love playing tennis
and watching Dennis!

Joe Taberer (11)
Echelford Primary School

My Magic Box
(Based on 'Magic Box' by Kit Wright)

I will put in my box . . .
A dancing dotty dolphin diving into the deep blue sea.
A twisted tongue-tied tiger in my garden.
A cheeky monkey mumbling, munching apples and bananas.

I will put in my box . . .
A pretty pink, perfect sky.
My own blue, beautiful bubbled bath.
A beautiful white horse of my own.

I will put in my box . . .
An exciting, excellent, enjoyable baby elephant
And a whistle made of silver.
A wacky witch who flies around on her broomstick.
A perfect, pretty pet puppy
Who can sometimes be shy and hide behind the sofa.

I will put in my box . . .
The smell of green dew grass that's just been cut.
An excellent, exciting day being in Echelford.
I would like to be in water all the time
And swim like a mermaid.

My box is made from tiger skin, studded with some golden rings
And held by big waves.
I shall live in my box and shall enjoy when I can.

Chloe Boon (10)
Echelford Primary School

What Is . . . A Ghost?

A ghost is a ghostly menace,
It is a transparent misty spectre.

It is a hideous moaning phantom,
A ghost is a soft white duvet floating the corridors.

It is a dead spirit,
It is your worst nightmare.

Tom McNab (10)
Echelford Primary School

My Magic Box
(Based on 'Magic Box' by Kit Wright)

I will put in my box . . .

A dancing dolphin diving into the deep blue sea.
The first waddling walk of my baby cousin.
The taste of a home-made cake.

I will put in my box . . .

The ability to fly places.
To fly over the tidy treetops.
Seeing the stripy tigers down low.

I will put in my box . . .

The smell of the fresh air.
The taste of a cooked pizza.
To see the open world.

My box is made of . . .

Sparkling silver and glittering gold
With a touch of wood on the bottom.

My box is decorated with . . .

Delicate diamonds on the lid
With shiny silk on the bottom.
The furriest tiger fur.

I shall skate in my box
Until the ice has melted.

Molly Nash (9)
Echelford Primary School

What Is A Ghost

A ghost is a translucent stream of milk.
It is a ghastly menace.
It's a big, white see-through shirt.
It's a book filled with clean white paper.
A ghost is a floating, growling, fluffy cloud.

Shayla Ash (10)
Echelford Primary School

Kennings Car

Wall-basher
  Lorry-crasher
    Petrol-guzzler
     Man-puzzler
      Rubbish-tipper
    Road-wipper
   Bus-crusher
Highway-rusher.

Matthew Rogers (11)
Echelford Primary School

Elephant

How tiny is a child unto the elephant's eye?
Head like a marble that glows over nigh.

Body lemon, all yellow and round.
Legs like twigs that stand on the ground.

Arms like toothpicks that stick in the lemon toes
Like bulbs that stick on the feet.

Ross Grant (9)
Echelford Primary School

Kennings Car

Drag-racer
  Car-chaser
    Race-winner
      Petrol-dinner
      Engine-blower
     Bumper-tower
    Central-heater
Breakdown-beater.

Harry Jackman (10)
Echelford Primary School

Best Things

Very late nights,
Bright morning light,
A baby lion cub,
Arsenal football club,
Multicoloured fish,
A full dish,
The taste of custard,
Smell of mustard,
Strawberries and ice cream,
A loud, loud scream,
Television for two hours,
The smell of true flowers,
The softness of a soft pillow,
The taste of marshmallow,
I read the Secret Seven,
But I prefer to go to Devon.

Ellouise Holley (10)
Echelford Primary School

Giraffe

I'm like a fly,
To a giraffe's eye.
An ant as small as a dot,
A giraffe can see a lot.
To a giraffe my leg's a dinky twig,
An ox is the size of a pig.

To a giraffe a car's a shoe,
A chair would be a footrest.
A giraffe's skin as smooth as silk,
Her neck too tall to reach the milk.
A poor giraffe must get very lonely
In the air all day.

Tasmin Arnould (9)
Echelford Primary School

Ox

To an ox an ant is a speck of dust
Moving in the wind.
An ox's horns are like swords
Gazing steadily.
His eyes like bombs
Looking red and mean.
He's black like the darkness.
He charges fast
Like a fireball carrying its heavy load.

Nathan Keeley (8)
Echelford Primary School

Winter

Winter has come at last,
The snow is glistening on the trees.
I hear children playing,
Their hands are going to freeze.

All the animals are hibernating,
Underneath the cold and wet earthy ground.
I look and look for these slumbering creatures,
But they are nowhere to be found.

Jodie Knowles (10)
Echelford Primary School

Giraffe

How tiny is a child to a giraffe's eye?
Hair like a brown leaf
Shining through the air.
Head like a mushroom
Down in the ground.
Arms like sticks
From the big bushy trees.

Zoe High (9)
Echelford Primary School

Bandit The Badger

Bandit the badger was wicked and mean,
whenever he committed a crime he could never be seen.
Wherever he went and whatever he had done,
you can be sure he carried a gun.
He was really smooth,
and he liked to groove.

Bandit the badger was very slick
and lollypops he liked to lick.
Bandit the badger he liked to steal,
he was so busy he barely had a meal.
He was so fast,
it would never last.
Eventually he was caught
and he was distraught.

Bill Clack (9)
Echelford Primary School

Bull

A bull is as strong as 20 men
Charging at anything it glares at
As brown as a tree
Horns sharp as swords
As big as an elephant
As scary as zombies coming out of the ground
Horns sparkle in moonlight.

As powerful as a tank
Knocking anything in his path
Nothing stand in its way!

Elliot Bernath (9)
Echelford Primary School

Demon The Disgusting Dog

Demon the disgusting dog was always committing a crime,
But he always got away, just in the nick of time,
He smells like cheese and steals people's teas,
He really enjoyed biting knees.

Demon the disgusting dog always carried a gun,
But whenever the cops were there
He was always sucking his thumb.

Demon the disgusting dog sneaked in houses
And chased the rats,
But worst of all he killed the cats,
That Demon, the disgusting dog.

Demon the disgusting dog once ate a frog
His breath smelt like a smelly bog,
The frog he ate, it made him jump
He hit the floor with a great big bump.

Connor Christmas (9)
Echelford Primary School

The Bear

A bear is as fierce as fire.
As rough as a tyre.
So big he looks like a leafless tree.
The bear's teeth like sharp blades.
We are like ants to this enormous creature.
He will rip your skin off.
Like you do to a chicken leg.
This creature will squash your car like a tin can
With his bare hands.

Beware of the bear!

Shenice Baptiste (9)
Echelford Primary School

Sidney The Cat

Sidney was a silly cat,
He was strange, sly and very fat,
He was the king of criminals in the town,
He never ever let them down.

Sidney wasn't ever seen,
Never left a paw print where he'd been,
Ran around the streets by day,
And never left a hair astray.

Sidney was as black as night,
Gave everyone a terrible fright,
The town's people locked their doors,
In case he'd steal any more.

Carrie Lee Holman (10)
Echelford Primary School

Harry The Hyena

Harry the hyena is a daring one,
When there is a crime, he's already been and gone.
He is as fast as a jumbo jet
And hasn't even been to the vet.
He is really very spotty
And his laugh drives you potty.

He lives in the open plains
And he loves to play dangerous games.
He goes hunting far and near,
To catch a juicy deer.
At the end of the day
He shouts, 'Hooray!'

Michael Arbon (9)
Echelford Primary School

Matt The Mischievous Monkey

Matt the mischievous monkey is the fastest thing in the jungle,
He's slick and sly and no one could ever catch him,
He teases tigers and rides on lions, he pulls on elephants' ears.
People have tried to catch him but he's always out of sight.

Matt the mischievous monkey loves to be on TV,
Once, about a year ago, he became a famous monkey.
He was on 'I'm a Celebrity, Get Me Out Of Here!'
And guess what? He won. 'But how?' people said,
He chased them all out.

Matt the mischievous monkey is the fastest thing in the jungle,
He's slick and sly and no one has ever caught him,
He wrestles gorillas and always wins, he strangles snakes,
He races cheetahs and beats them every time.
Matt the mischievous monkey is the new king of the jungle.

Tyler Fraser-Coombe (10)
Echelford Primary School

Frightening Fox

The frightening fox is very bad,
All he does is make people sad,
He eats most of everybody's food,
When he's in a hungry mood.
He will go through your smelly bins
And lick the food off open tins.

The frightening, frightening, frightening fox,
You'll never find him in a box,
Nor under the sofa or on the chair,
Or sleeping with your teddy bear
These criminal foxes are really rare,
He has green eyes like a pear.

Katie Simms (9)
Echelford Primary School

Gorilla

How small unto the gigantic gorilla
Must big things look.
A five-storey high palm tree to climb
Is like reading a book.

A huge tree like a caulifower,
An enormous elephant,
A bed like a shoe,
A massive tree like a twig.

Jack Dunbar (8)
Echelford Primary School

I'd Love To Be Beckham

I'd love to be Beckham
Curl a ball around,
A goalie called Seaman
Who fell right to the ground.

I'd love to be Beckham
Score a fantastic goal,
In the World Cup final
Maybe I'll believe it.

I'd love to be Beckham
With that handsome face,
Have two children
And live in a palace place.

I'd love to be Beckham
With all that money
Spend it so I won't look funny.

Isaac Lyndsay (11)
Edgware Junior School

The Snow Angel

Twinkling, glistening all around
As a blanket of snow covers the ground
Birds singing at their best
As the snow angel lays down to rest

Her beauty I see as she lies on the ground
Shining white snow all around
She slowly drifts from sky to floor
Little by little, and then some more

I awoke next morning to find she had gone
I remember how she glistened and shone
But alas, no more is she
No more of her beauty will I see.

Priscilla Osoba (10)
Edgware Junior School

Alexander

A lexander is my name
L ike doing art
E njoy playing football, my best game
X mas is coming, I can't wait
A fter school I'm home late
N aughty I am when I can't get my way
D ad's at work so I can play
E ating is next, like
R abbit stew on my desk.

Alexander Zendra (8)
Edgware Junior School

Yellow Bella

Yellow Bella has blonde hair
She wears a scarlet jumper
That's baggy of course
But she is fair
She is as bouncy as a hare
No wonder she likes dollies
She says that lollies are bad
And if you eat them,
Monsters come to life,
You want to know why
She's called Yellow Bella?
She's the yellowest fellow.

Samantha Sivapragasam (9)
Edgware Junior School

Peace

World world
We must have peace.
The world needs to stop
Falling apart.
World world
We need to be
Like a family
And be together
For as long
As we live.

Runako Munyoro (8)
Edgware Junior School

My Dog

My dog is fat and furry
with big floppy ears

He is little but he can run fast
he won a race against me in the past

When I get in from school
he comes up to me, cuddles me

When it is wet he splashes me
in the puddles. His bark is funny

And he likes to play in parks
and he likes to play catch

He has dark brown eyes just like me
and a big, black, shiny nose

When I call he comes running
with his fast little legs,

And when the man puts the letters
through he jumps up at them.

Rosie Watts (9)
Edgware Junior School

Summer

S ummer is nice in a place like a farm
U mbrellas we don't need, so leave it calm.
M ore sunshine,
M ore poetry line.
E verything is nice and hot,
R ainbows we won't see, even inside a pot.

Faisal Iqbal (9)
Edgware Junior School

Friends

When your friends are kind to you,
you must be the same as well.

Always choose a good one
not a bad.

If you choose a bad friend
you will be bad as well.

A good friend will put you
on the right path.

If you choose a bad one
you will follow the wrong path.

Friend is for need
friend is forever.

Sara Failey (10)
Edgware Junior School

In The Woods

In the woods there's lots of trees
with green, red and orange leaves.
I would go in the woods at night
Because I would get such a fright.

With shadows, animals and creepy spiders
Crawling all along beside us.

I hope you never have to go there
'Cause you will end up
With creepy crawlies in your hair.

Ronnie Creed (8)
Edgware Junior School

Snow, Snow

Snow, snow
Where are you?
Up in the sky
Down on the ground?
Snow, snow
Are you going to melt?

Snow, snow
Are you going to play with me?
Play rumble tumble
With me all day long

When the sun comes
You'll melt away
And you'll be gone
Without saying goodbye
I'm going to miss you snow

Goodbye snow
See you another day.

Kundai Rusike (8)
Edgware Junior School

Winter

Winter is the coldest season
Children eating candy canes and sweets
Making chilly winds blow
Snowmen are building up on the streets.

Children throwing snowballs
Having lots of fun
Indoors or outdoors
Because Christmas has begun.

Maariya Parkar (9)
Edgware Junior School

Equality

In my world we're all equal
Doesn't matter what colour we are
We're all one big family
Everyone should be treated equally
In one great harmony
Colour of skin doesn't matter
People with glasses doesn't mean they're different
Everyone is the same inside
What is inside is what matters
There is no such thing as the best or the worst
We're all good at something
Religion should not separate people.

In my game there are no winners or losers
Everyone wins
Everyone should play together
No one should be left out
A mixture is always the best
A song made by only playing white notes on the piano,
Makes the same sound as a song played by black notes
The better sound comes from the song,
That is played by both white and black notes.
Do not judge a book by its cover.

Everything is equal
Equality rules.

Salva Ravan (10)
Edgware Junior School

Snowy Day

The sky is cloudy.
The grass is crunchy.
The wind is icy.
The snow is falling.

This is the month of January.
The rooftops are snowy.
The windows are frosty.
The snow is falling.

The wind is blowing
The blizzard is freezing.
People are falling.
I think the snow is lovely.

Halima Djeraoui (8)
Edgware Junior School

Tidy Up

Tidy tidy give me a rest
because I do not think it is best.

Tidy tidy I cannot find my vest
because my brother is such a pest.

Tidy tidy my dad has a hairy chest
and my mum is the best.

Tidy tidy my bedroom is a mess
and I am going to wear my dress.

Jade Lafferty (9)
Edgware Junior School

Cyclone

Cyclone crashing,
Cyclone mad,
Cyclone angry, furious, howling,
Sucking like a Hoover.
Cyclone deafening,
Cyclone gigantic.
Cyclone twirling
Round and round
Demolishing everything in sight.
Destroying walls,
Houses and trees.
Who will see it next?
Let us see!

Flynt Nicoll-Coker (8)
Edgware Junior School

My Brilliant Friend

My friend is brilliant at football.
My friend is brilliant at maths.
My friend is brilliant at riding horses.

My friend is fantastic at English.
My friend is great at netball.
My friend is good at basketball.

My friend is fond of reading.
My friend is brilliant at tennis.
My friend is dazzling at stories.

Eniola Dare (9)
Edgware Junior School

Seasons

Winter, summer, autumn, spring,
children running in the wind.
Cold, snowy and sunny people
find it really funny.
When it is raining,
people are playing.
When it is sunny,
people are running.
When the rainbow is out
all the people stare and shout.
Sunny weather's the best,
it's got more light than the rest.

Lubna Mahirban (11)
Edgware Junior School

Through That Door

Through that door
Are lots of fireworks.
Through that door
Is a big waterfall.
Through that door
Is a house on fire.
Through that door
Are lots of people.
Through that door
Is a land full of snow.
Through that door
Is a colourful rainbow.

Josh McCormick (10)
Edgware Junior School

My Noisy Class

Alexander likes to play ball
Benji's always messing around
Cealigh's talking to her friends
Damini's chatting to the rest of the class
Diego talks Portuguese
Haider's reading a book aloud
Kundai likes to sing and play
Muhamud is crazy every day
Tempany likes to jog and run
Georgie likes to have some fun
Runako likes to call people 'babies'
Ronnie's very quiet
And this is my class
And they're very noisy.

Rhys Ellis (7)
Edgware Junior School

Litter Off The Pavement

Litter off the pavement please
We don't want the world all messy.
So get up and clean up just like me.
If you see anybody dropping litter on the pavement
Tell the person you must not drop litter on the pavement,
Because do you want the world all messy?
So just do the right thing.
You can surprise your mum and dad
And you can teach them all about litter off the pavement.

Amber Sedki-Farag (7)
Edgware Junior School

A Magical Time

I ran
away from the house
away from the shouting
away from the cars, roads and smoke
of time and life
I ran, into the woods
the cool, green woods,
there is not a sound.
Sunlight flickers through the lush beech leaves.
I slow my pace to a stride, a walk, a tiptoe.
I emerge into a clearing.
There by a crystal clear lake,
I halt.
A doe comes silently to the other side of the lake,
her fawn body seeming to float on slender legs.
She looks straight at me with her deep brown eyes.
I cannot move.
She holds me, locked in her gaze.
We stand, staring at each other for a long time.
Maybe minutes, maybe hours,
standing, staring.
Then she turns and disappears back into the woods.
I turn too.
What a wonderful moment,
a magical time.

Grace Harrison (11)
Highfield Primary School

The Tramp

I scavenge through the bags and bins,
Only finding empty boxes and tins,
My heart fills with great dismay,
No chance at all to shout *hooray!*

As I walk into the next street,
My bare skin burns in the heat,
How I long for something to eat,
Anything good, vegetables or meat.

When people pass they stare,
Without the slightest care,
For six months I have lived alone,
But I have never moaned.

I am sure I am going to die,
And I ask myself *why!*
Why did I find no food to cover my bones?
And there is no place like home, *sweet home!*

Rahul Thakrar (11)
Holland House School

Swimming

    Little strokes, big strokes
It does not matter what,
    Long lengths, short lengths
It still makes you hot,
    Jump and dive
It is still all swimming!

    Relax on a float and kick your legs
Watch the birds fly in the sky,
    And watch the clouds as they go by
Watch the flowers in sparkling drops,
    Make waves, make ripples
But please don't stop swimming!

Phyllis Sowah (10)
Holland House School

The Wealth Of The Mountains

There once were two brothers
And their father, who was the king.
One brother was strong and wealthy
While the other was much older than he.

One repulsive day, death caught the king,
The advisor told his majesty's sons, what were due,
That the king's wealth of the mountains
Would be given to either of the two.
It was announced that they would race each other.
The second horse to pass the finish line,
Would be the victor and receive the wealth of the mountains.

Thus it began, they rode slowly on their horses.

Fifty years later they were struggling with old age,
'Let us battle, it shall be fair, one of us shall rise to the heavens
And one of us shall receive the wealth of the mountains.'

Thus they fought until blood concealed them
And so did the dismay!

One was finally victorious but died the following day.

Gopi Sivakumaran (11)
Holland House School

A New Lesson

I had a bad day today.
Nothing at all went my way.
I woke up on the wrong side of the bed
And by the time I'd washed, I had a spinning head.

In class I didn't do anything right,
Because I hadn't revised last night.
I was told off and started to cry
Therefore my eyes were no longer dry.

During break Mary Jane gave me a hard time.
I'm also having trouble writing this rhyme.
By the end of school, I looked like a fool.
I had lunch in my hair, now that was not fair!

By the time I arrived, I was deprived
Of all my sanity and civilisation.
And it all came out, in my frustration.

I pulled a tuft of grass
And smashed a valuable glass.
I slammed the door
And banged on the floor.

But now I am grounded, I have found
That life is not free; nor is it easy!

Shenal Shah (11)
Holland House School

The Shadow

Silently drifting through the wood,
I could have caught him, I could, I would.
Making the largest trees look small,
The shadow reflected on the wall.
Why was he here, when and how?
I asked myself under a leaning bough.

The night broke, in flooded light.
The shadow had vanished along with the night.

'Shadow, Shadow, where have you gone?
Please come back, and don't be long!'

'Shadow, Shadow, where are you now?
Please come back, you'll cause a row!'

'You silly Shadow, you've gone away,
So after all, I don't want you to stay!'

Caitlin Pinner (10)
Holland House School

Misery

I finally realise what it's like to be
A person full of misery.
I never knew that it would be like this,
I miss my old life - so full of bliss.
Some people cope, but no, not me
I want my life back, my life of glee.

A car crash - someone on a phone,
Because of that I'm now alone,
It's really hard, every day a struggle,
I miss my father and his warm cuddle.
And just because of a bump on the head,
I now know how it feels to be dead.

Sarah Chaplin (11)
Holland House School

A Sunday Afternoon

A normal Sunday, Mum is cooking a roast.
The dinner of all we love the most,
But this afternoon was destined to be
Somewhat different for my family and me.

My brother was watching England play football.
He was frustrated, angry and upset,
As Michael Owen was fouled and missed his shot.
Everyone was desperate for the referee to point to the spot.

It was the European final
We were all desperate to win.
The final whistle and dinner were approaching fast.
'Come on England, win!'

My brother was starving,
My dad was carving,
Everyone was licking their lips.
You could go and snatch the food right now
But that would be impolite.

Alexander Lewis (10)
Holland House School

I Am Alone

I am alone.
I repeat it again and again,
Breathing upon the window
In my rundown house.
Shedding tears, but no one cares.

I am alone.
An orphan without a guardian,
A child without a childhood; friends or family.
Every day I watch the world go by
Thinking about the future not the past;
Of the day when I shall be remembered.

I am alone.
My life is a cycle of pain and sorrow,
Never imagining tomorrow.
I cherish the only possession I have
A photograph of my parents' marriage.
This photo shows me that life and love
Once reigned in this house.

I am alone.
I've abandoned hope,
My dreams forfeited.
I've lost the battle,
I wish to die while others plead to live.
I lie here lingering until my permanent slumber.

Naikee Kohli (10)
Holland House School

Just To Please A Lover

Love is a mystery
It will come and go,
In the time of a flutter of lovebird's long lashes,
Vanity creeps over the unaware
Just to please a lover.

Love is joyful,
A rose never can smell as sweet as when given by a lover,
A sweet but futile kiss, given on a powdered cheek,
Powdered by vanity
Just to please a lover.

Love is a beautiful thing
Given to those who least expect it,
Hushed by their lover's call,
They prepare though unaware it is vanity all,
Just to please a lover.

Love is a feeling, strong and bold
Forever inside you waiting, waiting to come out.
Everyone has a chance, you have to hold on,
They do everything they can, even vanity,
Just to please a lover.

Kate Freedman (10)
Holland House School

I Needed

I needed a coat
I needed a toy boat
I needed a holiday in Geneva
I needed a kit
So that I could knit
I needed a message receiver.

I needed some plates
I needed a mate
I needed a good hot, warm meal
How about chicken?
Potatoes or peas?
Or what about carrots and veal?

I needed a pan
I needed a fan
I needed a peaceful old rest
We're visiting Grandpa's
Tomorrow? So soon?
Now I have to be at my best!

I needed a break
I needed to bake
I needed to escape from my brother
So I said, 'Oh Lord, what shall I do?'
I know!
I'll just ask my mother!

Elio Elia (10)
Holland House School

Colours

Red is the colour of danger,
Showing you where you shouldn't go.
Green is the colour of envy
And tells you when you can go.

Yellow is as bright as the sun,
And as sour as a lemon.
Blue is when you're feeling cool,
Or the sky below the heavens.

Orange is the colour when you're feeling calm,
And also the colour of gold.
Purple is the colour when you're happy inside,
Or when you are feeling bold.

White is the colour of Heaven's halos,
And is very, very plain.
Black is the colour of the end of your life
Or when you start all over again.

Georgia Sears (10)
Holland House School

Poppy

Through the wind and through the night
I see my friends fall down with fright

I wish that the wars would stop
So the men don't drop.

The wars were bloody
And the men were muddy.

That is why we remember
The 11th of November.

Joshua Alfred Gibbons (10)
Longmead Primary School

Pollution

Night and day, I stay and think,
Night and day, I cannot blink,
I see people die and cry,
I see people that do not try,
People drink, people eat,
People do not think about the meat,
I know the solution,
Stop the pollution.
The water that we drink is from the sea,
So tell me, what shall it be?
Pollution is everywhere,
Yet people do not care.
People will laugh and dance,
Stand up and take a chance.
If you believe
Then you will see what we can achieve!

Luul Hussein (11)
Longmead Primary School

My Sister

When I get up from my bed,
I bang my head.

My alarm goes off,
I trip over my sock.

I shout for my sister
Because I really miss her,
So I rush to kiss her.

She's the bestest friend I've ever had,
If I had to choose between her and a lad,
I would choose my sister.

Sorath Soomro (10)
Longmead Primary School

How To Kill A Mocking Bird

How to kill a mocking bird,
It's easier said than done.
Chase it round the field,
It's torture more than fun.

How to kill a mocking bird,
Don't try it or you might
Wake up in the morning
And get a terrible fright!

How to kill a mocking bird,
It's all about truth or dare,
Catching it and eating it,
Now that's not very fair.

We all gather round,
All in a herd,
We all speak together,
On how to kill a mocking bird.

Frankie Denslow (11)
Longmead Primary School

How To Start A Poem

How do you start a poem?
I really don't know
All I can think of is a video game.

I know, I'll write a poem about cars.
No, no, how about . . . dogs!
No, how about dinos?
Yeah, I'll do that.
Umm, what do I know about dinos?
Umm, well umm, that's a hard one.
Ding! Ding! Line up.

Elliott Barker (9)
Longmead Primary School

Dancing Queen

I'm a dancing queen,
I have a big television screen.
I'm a dancing king
And I can sing.
We dance and sing
And the door goes ding.
All our neighbours like to join in,
So we put them all in the bin.

Uma Begum (9)
Longmead Primary School

Loving U

L ove is a feeling
O n and in your heart
V ery, very special
I t's inside and out
N ever going to stop
G oing on forever.

U love people and they love U.

Kayleigh Brown (10)
Longmead Primary School

About Jack

There once was a boy called Jack
He had a hairy back
He showed it off
The girls coughed
And that was the end of Jack.

Amy Kelvey (10)
Longmead Primary School

The Winning Team Zeo

In a football team called Zeo,
their leader was a very good hero.
They were facing the ten team trio,
where there was a chap called Rio.
They were worse off than a lady called Mellano,
who was sent to Hell,
because she said nothing well.

Then the two faced off,
leaving nothing but dust.
They played and played,
the goal post started to rust,
the keeper woke from dawn to dusk.
He couldn't move, the team trip lost,
they swallowed their pride
and walked home exhausted.

Amelio Ramkalawan (11)
Longmead Primary School

In The Cauldron

In the cauldron vegetables go,
In the cauldron bubbles glow
Green and grey the bubbles splat
And my black cat is called Matt.
Breast of chicken, and legs too
My black cat needs the loo.
Triple trap, spin and double
Fire burn and water splat
Throw in snakes and frogs' spawn too
I would love to sing to you.
Throw in heads and chopped up beds
I will chop off some heads.
Trash and smash everyone's big toe
And love to sing, 'Ho, ho, ho!'
Triple trap, spin and double
Fire burn and water splat.

Emma Ashford (10)
Longmead Primary School

The Hunter

Running through the forests,
During the night,
There was no sun,
There was no light.

Will he kill a fox,
Or maybe a deer,
He's very, very brave
And has no fear.

Running through the trees,
Past the honey bees,
Be careful of the lair,
Because there is a bear.

Hunting's his favourite thing,
He can't hunt when it's bright,
He only hunts
During the night.

The worst thing
Is a wolf's bite,
Not a bee's sting,
But hunting to a hunter
Is his favourite thing.

Hollie Ryder (10)
Longmead Primary School

Days Of The Week

Monday go swimming
Tuesday go to school
Wednesday go out the front
Thursday go shopping
Friday have a party
Saturday stay in bed
Sunday sit on the sofa and watch TV.

Hannah Gardner (9)
Longmead Primary School

I See Hair On The Floor

When my mum picks me up after school
And at home when we get in the hall
My dogs jump up at me and my mum.
When I go up the stairs I hum,
As I go in my room
And an hour later I hear a boom.
It's my sister next door.
Then I hear a roaring sound,
It sounded like a hound.
I went downstairs
And there were hairs
All over the floor
And I went through the front room door.
I see my dad in his chair
And again on the floor
I see hair.

Zara Thorn (9)
Longmead Primary School

Spring

Spring is my favourite season.
Because . . .
It is lovely,
The way the buds open,
Like inviting the Queen.
The beautiful flowers,
So pretty and bright,
Are not there in winter,
Oh! annoying winter,
Don't even let us keep these flowers,
You keep all the frost with you
To wipe out the flowers,
You are so unfair!

Ambika Natesan (10)
Reddiford School

Cinderella

My father divorced and married again,
To an attractive lady in the latest trend.

She wasn't as appealing and courteous as she looked,
She made me wash, scrub, mop and cook.

Her two hideous daughters were ideal to their mother,
Proud, vain, never had a care or a bother.

As I swept and swept the dusty floors,
My sisters ran in and out of doors.

They had been invited to a magnificent ball,
To the dance with the prince in the grand hall.

They combed their hair as flat as a flounder,
It made their head look rounder and rounder.

I wept and wept until I saw something bright,
It looked like a magical blaze of light.

'I am your fairy godmother and I have come to help you.'
I looked at her in shock wondering if that was true.

'If you bring me a few items you shall go to the ball!
They are two mice, a pumpkin and an overall.'

I obeyed all her orders and in the flick of an eye,
She turned them into a carriage, coachmen
And the most stunning, striking dress.

I stepped into the golden carriage
And rode to the palace gazing at the pleasant partridge.

I caught the prince's eye and danced away,
But when it was time to go I had to say.

I ran to the carriage as fast as I could,
Leaving the glass slipper on the stair's shiny wood.

The next day the prince came to our spotless house
And tried my glass slippers into my sisters' feet.

Their feet were too broad,
As it fitted onto Cinderella's feet wedding bells poured.

Shobana Sivalingam (10)
Reddiford School

The Lost Girl

Her life was like a dusty book
Being ignored wherever she glanced
She was cursed with her cover the pages she owned.
The features she was upon were guilt.
All she requested was a normal beginning, a middle and end
Was that too much to ask?
When the people looked at her they said,
'Yuck! That thing has to go.'
They said it so often again and again
It was torment to my ears
She chose to walk alone on this dirty path
All she wanted was freedom from these crooked puppet strings
She wished and she wished
Some say she wished too hard
Some say she wished too long
Until she woke up one autumn's day to see that she was gone.

Mustafaen Kamal (9)
Reddiford School

My Dog

My dog is like a fuse box,
Always tearing up socks;

He loves going for walks,
Chasing the cats and birds, which he stalks;

While playing games he happily licks,
But doing my homework he sadly kicks;

His favourite thing is chasing balls and twigs,
And when he catches one, he happily dances a jig.

Priya Patel (10)
Reddiford School

Fireworks

All the fireworks dancing and glistening in the dark night sky.
Zooming rockets shooting up so high.
Some showers of twinkling stars falling from the shrouded black sky.
They all have the colours of a clown.
Sonic FX screamers screeching, crying like witches.
Roman candles look like trees in an orchard
Dropping their petals and beautiful lime apples.
First the sky looks black, dull and boring.
But when the twirling, whirling, swirling, fizzing
And whizzing fireworks come they brighten up the sky.
They look like beautiful unfolding buds.
Children playing with sparklers,
Their little flaming hot sparks dancing.
All the colours like rosy red, brilliant blue and gorgeous green.
The Catherine wheels are like orange,
Glistening and spinning marigolds.

Conor O'Brien (10)
Reddiford School

The Falling Star

It was a dark, cold night
In a twinkle, I saw a bright light shooting in the sky.
What could it be?
Could it have been a falling star?
I did not know.
But I just closed my eyes and made a wish
I did not open for a very long time
And when I opened my eyes, a bright light blinded me
It was the sun!
I am sure I saw the falling light last night
As my wish came true!

Shruti Dorai (9)
Reddiford School

My Pet Hamster

My hectic hamster is like a gang,
Steering into trouble,
His greediness is more than average,
Always eating double.

He has a motor fixed inside,
Speeding up and down,
His silky skin is beige and white,
With a touch of brown.

His razor-sharp teeth are like a snake's,
Gnawing at his block,
Yesterday he stole my glove,
And my other sock.

His glistening eyes are a copy of a cat's,
Sharp and ever so catching,
Apart from a cat these pair of eyes,
On an animal would never be matching.

His puny paws are those of a bear's,
Ever so painful when slashed,
His take-down rampage is very positive,
You do not want to get bashed.

His cute, miniature face is like a lie,
The trick within his smile,
But when you creep nearer he lashes out,
Trying to heal the pain? It'll take a while!

Lawrence Xu (10)
Reddiford School

Dragons

Dragons come from out of the sun, waiting to make their kill,
For they and the sun come to make one
To bring fire to the world
The world,
The world,
To bring fire and heat to the world.

When they come down they fight for the crown,
To rule over the world,
Their bright blazing colour,
Makes everything shudder,
Even the setting sun.

Then they fly up so high,
Where the birds glide,
In the sky,
To bring fire and heat to the world,
The world,
The world,
To bring fire and heat to the world.

Niral Bharat (10)
Reddiford School

Animals

A nts scurrying up and down
N ightingales singing a joyful tune
I nteresting pufferfish bubbling
M ammals great and mammals small
A rachnids crawling around your house
L izards, reptiles that look so mean
S abre-toothed tigers, now are extinct.

Rishi Peshavaria (10)
Reddiford School

A Firework Extravaganza

Fizzing fireworks shining bright
Zooming rockets fly to fight
Sparkling they are gunpowder stars
They shoot so high they reach Mars

Listen as they explode and blow,
Please come over for a magical show
Sonic FX screamer crying like mad
It's like a baby wailing oh so sad
Majestic rockets boom and unfold

Wondrous sights for all to behold
Cold and numb are our fingers and toes
But today is the night that no one moans
The grand finale is now here
Everyone shouting an enchanting cheer

Emerging elegant fireworks
Like a bomb from the First World War
Everything blows up just past your door.

Rishil Bhikha (9)
Reddiford School

A Winter's Day

As the cold winter settles the snow starts to fall.
The winter settling for a long winter's night.
Snow falls white never melts, for a night.
Flowers are frozen day by day.

The snow is as white as a cloud's.
But more cold outside than inside.
The birds are no more for they have fled.
Feared and horrible winter has now appeared!

Robbie Singh (10)
Reddiford School

No More Gingerbread Man!

There was an old lady who baked a gingerbread man,
He jumped out of the oven and scarpered across the floor
And off he ran, the gingerbread man,
Out of the wide open door.

The old woman and the old man,
The cow and the horse all called,
'Stop and come back little man.'
He shouted, 'No way, come and catch me if you can.'

He ran with all his might,
'Come back, you look like a tasty meal.'
He shouted, 'Not without a fight.'
'Come on, let's make a deal.'

He came to a river and met a clever fox
And he never looked back,
'I will help you cross,' beamed the fox,
He agreed and jumped on his tail.

So they set off on their sail when the fox said,
'Jump onto my back or you'll fall onto our track.'
Then he said, 'Jump onto my nose
So you don't get squirted by a hose.'

After a wonderful wild ride
They reached the other side
He flung him into the air without a care
And as quick as a flash, he munched him up.

Rikhil Shah (9)
Reddiford School

Heart Of Evil

Death was close,
The dark lord waited,
Waited for news,
Spies returning to his barren land.

The dark lord waited,
Waited for the great battle,
Mace down,
Ready for battle,
His heart burning with hatred,
All good exploded into flames of death.

The dark lord waited,
Waited for the sun to be banished
Into the depths of Hell,
A perfect place for darkness to breed.

Finally the hour arrives,
The dark lord moving into battle,
His silver and black armour shining,
His enemies drowned in a sea of terror,
As they stared into his empty eye sockets,
His demons cried triumphantly,
In the great hall they feasted on blood,
Shining on in the moonlight,
Wicked laughter echoing through the night sky.

For the dark lord there was no sleep,
He felt no satisfaction,
For his wish is to dominate the world
With his heart of evil.

Rupen Patel (9)
Reddiford School

The Crimson Blossom Tree

The tree whistling like a whistle,
The shape of a pure heart
And the blushing of soft cotton.

The blossoms collapsing like crimson snow
The breeze of pink fireworks
The tree welcoming handy, stiff branches

The breezing wind kissing against my face,
Spreading like a heap of piled strawberries
She catches with her branch
And then catches it just like a ball.

The blooms of reddish crimson blossoms,
Is the best of all kinds,
It smells just like rose scent filled with cushion air
And the sea-coloured tree is best of all.

Niththilan Sritharan (8)
Reddiford School

The Victorians

The Victorian children are very poor,
They have to collect money from rich folks' door.

The families are living in one big room,
The children come home with terrible doom.

A man came along and thought it was wrong.
He cheered them up by singing them a song.

For a change the poor have respect,
Unlike the poor the rich had a very bad effect!

Ankit Patel (10)
Reddiford School

Pencil Sharpener

A sharpener's an enemy
Teasing you to a point which hurts
A deceitful friend
Leading a pencil to its doom.

When a pencil looks ugly
And needs a new look
It will turn to its companion
Its cunning friend Sharpener.

The sharpener is a hunter
Seeking for its prey
Prowling around sneakily
Devouring pencil after pencil.

When the sharpener sees its victim
It gives it pointers for a new look
Then slowly it demolishes its prey
The helpless and gullible pencil.

The sharpener's technique is very convincing
As the trustful pencil doesn't suspect it
Its routine is like a firework being lit
When the fire reaches the powder, *kaboom!*

There the pencil lies
Resting on its deathbed
Confused and foolish
It will never ever trust a sharpener

So it starts all over again . . .

Shivana Sood (10)
Reddiford School

Three Toa Tales

In the darkness he awaits,
Giving weak enemies terrible fates.
Makuta sends his brother to sleep,
And makes his brother's sons weep.
He casts a shadow of darkness,
And creates a terrible mess.
But Makuta was tricked,
For six heroes of Mata Nui butt kicked.

Toas, Lewa, Tahu,
Gali, Pohatu,
Onua and Kopaka,
Their mission to protect the turaga.
Swords, claws and axes,
Kept them on Makuta's tracks.
To find the golden masks,
But to do so they had to complete terrible tasks.

They had to defeat the
Bohrok, Rahkshi,
The Barag twins,
And the Rahi. But still the Toa had unlimited wins.
When they defeated these twin,
They thought they had another win.
But this was just the beginning . . .

They turned into the Nuva,
But not just the Toa.
The Bohrak changes just as well,
Into the Kal. And they took the Toa symbols and the Toa fell.
Stronger masks,
Devastating tasks.
They hunted down the Bohrak,
But the Toa would not flock.
In a cave they found both twin,
But they thought they could not win.

The mask of time,
Named Vahi. Given to the Tahu by the great Vakama
And its power was fine.
Controlling everything, Tahu wanted to slow enemies to battle,
To make the enemy slow as cattle.

He slowed time for the others to get the symbols,
But the Bohrak would not be broken by Pohatu's coals.
They gave the Kal their power,
But the Kal would not devour.
They boosted the risk,
But the Kal was destroyed in a whisk.
What did Makuta have in store next?

The Rakshi's mission was to prevent them
From finding the Toa of light,
And without a fight.

Jamie Tanna (9)
Reddiford School

My Bed

My comfy little bed
Sits in my room
Patiently waiting to be slept in.
The purple sheets cover
My squashy and bouncy mattress

My blanket envelops me like a cocoon
Thick and soft
How I can't wait till bedtime

A place where my dreams come alive
And my thoughts go wild
The warmth of my bed
Makes me never want to get up
As I snuggle under the covers
Hugging my cuddly teddy bears
Wishing I could stay in bed forever!

Misha Mansigani (11)
Reddiford School

The Night Sky

As the cobalt clouds sway along the chrome, yellow moon,
The dingy blue clouds make a reflection upon the azure-blue sea.
As the yellow moon lurched in the sky
It made a pitch-black reflection
Which made you look like a massive ogre.
All the minute golden yellow sun spots
Make the world a shiny place.
This minute star enraptures the scientists
When they go to sleep there are cold clouds outside
Looking like a polar bear's riding in through winds.
As the quiet astronomers listen to the wind howl like the whistling wolf,
They get a shiver.
The yellow, circular ball shines upon the blue sea
Which looks like a football on the pitch.
As the tawny moon goes to sleep,
The ever colossal football wakes up from its woody dreams.

Haran Devakumar (10)
Reddiford School

The Cherry Tree

The trunk and branches look like swills of Cadbury's chocolate.
I feel like stopping and having a bite.
At night-time the tree was glowing in the moonlight
and the branches were blowing.
Suddenly I felt like it was snowing fluffy candyfloss.
The blossom like mini roses in the sky.
The colour of sweet strawberry bubblegum as the days fly by.
One end of the magnificent tree is by my friend
and the other with little me.
The wind is kissing my face.
Clouds are running a race.
By the cherry tree it is such an overgrown place.

Amber-Rose Blogg (8)
Reddiford School

The Clouds Of Speed

A head turns with amazing speed
And yells, 'We are going to need,
A lot of haste,
To quickly get out of this base!'
It is the clouds of speed.

Suddenly panic breaks out,
'We haven't the time to run about!'
What was a speck, is now a dot,
A high-pitched scream comes from a cot.
It is the clouds of speed.

Nearer and nearer, here it comes,
The billowing clouds and beating drums,
As fear sets in, they arm themselves,
As the ringers sound the warning bells.
It is the clouds of speed.

Just one boy was left,
Who eked out a living by theft.
The thunder of hooves comes to an end,
As the last few come round the bend.
The boy could not bear,
To look at what stood there.
It is the clouds of speed.

He took a hand away from his face
And slapped himself in disgrace.
For what stood in front of him was neither man nor bear,
But a fine and beautiful chestnut mare.
Following closely behind,
Were others who looked as gentle and as kind.
It is the clouds of speed.

The boy may have lost the race,
To escape from the comfort of his base.
But he has, in fact, won the race,
To stare fright right in the face.
It is the clouds of speed.

Dominic Dichen (11)
Reddiford School

Ice

The southern wind hissed
Across the valleys,
What was water
Now is ice.

The sweet rippling
Water was
The imprisoned grass,
Now tender green.

Clear and ringing,
No sunny spells,
Where boys are sliding,
With chilly toes.

Each stick is covered
With stalk and blade,
With winter's coldness
Crystals are made.

Worms and ants,
Flies, snails and bees,
They're part of nature
But now they freeze.

Oh it's so sad,
Their eyes glare,
Each fish stares,
How sad we're going to die.

In dread let all be well.
Wide, watery home,
At night shall solid
Ice become.

Kishan Patel (10)
Reddiford School

A Seagull

Strolling along the deserted beach,
I heard a loud, high-pitched screech.
It was coming from the sky,
I saw a seagull flying high.
Scavenging for people's leftover fish and chips,
If he didn't have a beak he would lick his lips.
People say a seagull is a pest,
But people don't think, they just guess.
Seagulls are kind creatures,
Seagulls have strong features.
His eye is like a shiny black bead.
A seagull soars with incredible speed.
When a seagull chooses his fish,
He says to himself, 'Mmm, this is delish!'
He sits on the shore and scoffs it down,
Not making a complaint or wearing a frown.
My poem about a seagull has come to an end,
I hope you now realise that a seagull is a friend.

Meera Relwani (10)
Reddiford School

What Am I?

A sly slitherer
A poisonous kisser
A scenery blender
A silent hisser
A careful slanderer
A stealthy attacker
A legless mover
An eye catcher
A spine shiverer
A blood chiller
A scaly mass
A death giver.

What am I?

Akash Alexander (11)
Reddiford School

Moon

Shining in the darkened night
Giving off a beautiful light

Waxing and waning, doing its own thing
Like a man who thinks he's king

That's what I think
There he sits, 'til it's time to sink

He floats in the ebony universe
And undoes every evil, bound curse

Up high in the silky, black sky
Hovering until it's time to die

There he levitates while he waits
All around him are his mates

By that I mean the twinkling stars
Except of course for his best friend Mars

What's he made of, I wonder
Magic, dust and raging thunder

He wears a night-cap on his head
Unfortunately he has no bed

The silky sky wraps him up warm
Until it's time to go at dawn

Sitting there in the lonely night
With nothing to do except give off light

Shining in the darkened night
Oh what an absolutely beautiful sight!

Zehra Saifuddin (11)
Reddiford School

The Strong Stone

The hard, rough and strong stone,
not as smooth as a white, clean bone,
or as spiky as a plastic, black comb,
but as hard and rough as any stone.

The hard, rough and strong stone,
not as soft as spongy foam,
or as big as the Millennium Dome,
but as hard and rough as any stone.

The hard, rough and strong stone,
not as money-making as having a loan,
or as cool as being in the zone,
but as hard and rough as any stone.

The hard, rough and strong stone,
not as clever as an electric phone,
or as bad as going through a groan,
but as hard and rough as any stone.

Olajide Olatunji (11)
Reddiford School

My Car

My car, my car
Can drive so far
With its golden colour.

The jeep, my jeep
Can leap so deep
Every other looks duller.

The road, the road,
Where traffic flowed,
One behind the other.

The horns, the horns
While everyone groans,
And says, 'Oh bother!'

Harin Bharadia (10)
Reddiford School

Words

They consist of letters from the alphabet,
They can turn into sentences in a flash of light,
They have powerful meanings, which you mustn't forget,
Some have difficult spellings, which are important to get right.
Words, words are all in my head,
Words, words have to be said.
Some are boring and some are amazing,
They have different classes like verbs and nouns.
Some of the endings are *ed, ly* and *ing*
You have to listen to words carefully
So you can hear all their sounds.
Words, words are all in my head,
Words, words have to be said.
Words are ingenious things,
They make everybody feel like kings
Because they have thought up a marvellous word
Which has never ever occurred.
Words, words are all in my head,
Words, words have to be said.

Nicola Gartenberg (11)
Reddiford School

Dragon

A ferocious breather
A flyer eager
An evil looker
As hot as a cooker
A sly warrior
An animal chomper
A dangerous killer
A fright filler
Eyes glow redder
Scales green and deader.

Akshay Baldota (10)
Reddiford School

The Teddy Bear

I love him
I hug him
I kiss him
I squeeze him

I play with him
spend the day with him
all night together

He calms me down
and stops a frown
appearing on my face.
Sometimes we play hide-and-seek
he hides in my suitcase

He's soft and fluffy
his name is Muffy,
Muffy the teddy bear

He comforts me
he clings to me
he plays with me
and stays with me

Forever he will be with me cos I love Muffy
the big brown bear.

Katie Walsh (11)
Reddiford School

Rain

The lights are all on, though it's just past midday,
There are no more indoor games we can play
No one can think of anything to say,
It rained all yesterday, it's raining today,
It's grey outside, inside me it's grey.

I stare out of the window, fist under my chin,
The gutter leaks, drips on the lid of the dustbin,
When they say, 'Cheer up,' I manage a grin,
I draw a fish on the glass with a sail-sized fin,
It's sodden outside, and it's damp within.

Matches, bubbles and papers pouring to the drains,
Clouds smother the sad laments from the trains,
Grandad says it brings on his rheumatic pains,
The moisture's got right inside my brains,
It's raining outside, inside me it rains.

Nisha Patel (10)
Reddiford School

Who Am I?

Below waters, salt and freshies glare.
Eye colours, yellow around black, like a bee.
As herbivores sip the water,
He will time his attack like a pro.
Then slowly, he wades towards it,
Success building in his eyes.
Jaws widen.
Sharp, red teeth glimmer in the sunshine.
And the poor thing is swallowed whole.
He makes his way back in the water.
Green and brown scales vanishing into calmness.
Ripples form and fade outwards.
And nobody knows he is there,
Hunting for more.

Shil Shah (11)
Reddiford School

Friends Are Here

Friends are here,
Friends are there,
Meant to be there, everywhere.

Friends, friends everywhere,
Let's do something together,
Scream, shout, run about
And let's have fun together.

Friends are there to help,
Friends are there to care,
Friends are there everywhere
Just make sure they're the best.

Friends come out,
Friends come in,
But you can rely on a friend
They are always there, friends.

Priyen Patel (10)
Reddiford School

Life

Life is not fair, life is not calm,
You can never hold it in the middle of your palm.

It just slips away and *poof* you are gone,
That's why you should use it wisely and take it seriously.

We face the toughest challenges, but there is
always light at the end of the tunnel.

So that's why they say life is not fair, life is not calm.

It just slips away and *poof* you are gone,
That's why you should use it wisely and take it seriously.

Feyi Onamusi (10)
Reddiford School

Who Am I?

I twist and turn like
A cat venturing into
Water struggling to grab its prey.
Some people get
Annoyed at me because
Of the mind-bending sounds
I make.

I like to eat delicious
Dirty, insanitary clothes
And love to drink soap.
If you disturb me while
I'm spinning like a dancer,
There will be a massive spillage
On the floor.

People use me a lot, if
They don't that means that
They are already too clean . . .
What am I?

Shamir Vekaria (10)
Reddiford School

Red

The glowing colour of my heart rushing through my body,
The sunset paints the sky with the burning colour deep inside me,
It unleashes my anger,
Within a blaze of fire, it brings heat to my body,
My pulse beats faster and faster,
I can feel my skin burning,
The blood flushes through me as I feel the adrenaline rush.

Shiv Mistry (11)
Reddiford School

Rocks

Rocks come in many different shapes and sizes
There are amethysts, rubies and sapphires.
Their textures can be rough or smooth,
It's up to you which one you choose.
Their colours can be any colour of the rainbow
Night-black, sea-blue, emerald-green or red.
When you've got a collection of them,
You will never get them out of your head.
Some as sharp as daggers,
Others smoother than silk,
Some rocks are bolt upright,
More natural rocks come on a tilt.
Diamonds are my favourite,
They're known to be a girl's best friend,
When I mention rocks to my brother, Tom,
It drives him round the bend.
Some as cold as stone,
Others as warm as the sun,
Some are as light as feathers,
Others weigh a ton.
So please start collecting rocks,
Then I hope you'll admire them as much as I do,
They're inspiring objects,
I hope you think so too.

Helen Farmer (11)
Reddiford School

Green!

Green is the long, lengthy, luscious grass.
Swaying in the wind.
Green is the leaf of a lotus,
Flapping like a bird's wings.
Green is the long, slimy seaweed,
Floating in the deep blue sea.
Green is the top of tall palm trees
Looking down at me.
Green is the colour of a Christmas tee,
On a cold, festive night
Decorated in baubles and tinsel
And the holy star at the top, oh, so shiny and bright.
Green is the colour that says,
'Don't stop, *go!*'
To the rushing traffic, which goes to and fro.
Green is the colour of organically grown, leafy
Vegetables, yum.
Full of vitamins and minerals,
Good for my tum!
Green is the colour of a camouflaged
Chameleon hiding in a bush,
Waiting for its prey,
A beetle, a spider, or a fly - whoosh!
Green is the beautiful, calm sea
In paradise
Which I look out at
Lying on the golden sand
Am I really here? To believe,
I have to look twice.

Janaki Kava (10)
Reddiford School

English

Handwriting has a gracious curve,
Layered and sprinkled with colourful sequins.
It flows well just like the ocean, aiding you to see the motion.
English is packed with punctuation,
Teachers nagging to make corrections.
All the rest proudly placed in the right order
Without being traced with a blood-red marker piercing the heart.

Boldly stands another aspect,
Similes like raging lions,
Descriptions so deep and metaphors like mini adventures,
Importing their quality into stories,
Helping needy and beady authors bring success into their dreary lives.

As I write long, passionate stories,
I think of many acrostic poems
Filling pages and pouring descriptions as a filling of salad cream.

Neha Shukla (10)
Reddiford School

A Roseate Cherry Tree

The rose cherry tree
has rosy blossom falling on me,
reminding me of winter
when the fluffy clouds appear.

The rose cherry tree
has flushed snow falling on me,
reminding me of the park
where dandelions play.

The rose cherry tree
has pink candyfloss falling on me,
reminding me of the salmon sunset
which appears then disappears.

The rose cherry tree
is like reddish cherries for me.

Darshali Shah (9)
Reddiford School

Writing Poems

When we write a poem
We have to have a mix.
Adjectives and adverbs,
We use so many tricks.

Metaphors and similes
Lighten up your rhyme,
You have to have it perfect
To make your poem shine.

We use alliteration
To bring the words together,
They glide across the page
And stay there forever.

Poems set emotions,
Feelings from inside,
They let you run wild with joy,
Or can bring a tear to your eye.

Anoli Mehta (10)
Reddiford School

Rain

I see rain
Trickling down the drain.

Dripping down my face,
Falling at a steady pace.

The roads are slippery,
Drivers can't see clearly.

Two little feet splashing a puddle,
Drenched birds gather in a huddle.

Slow clouds in the grey sky,
I wonder if the sun could be shy.

I'm indoors now sipping tea,
Warm and cosy watching TV.

Jemie Irukwu (9)
Reddiford School

The Seasons

The winter's shower of ice-cold snow,
The sprinkling white dust
Along the slithering valleys they go,
Gazing upon us.

The autumn's tattered leaves,
The crimson-coloured leaves all over the flower bed
Bringing a tremendous breeze,
As well as landing on my head.

Springtime is my birthday,
When daffodils pop out,
All of us say, 'Hooray!'
Oh spring is great throughout.

The summer's blazing heat,
Yeah! It's a holiday,
Making us eat,
It's come to summer's days.

Nirali Shah (8)
Reddiford School

Fireworks

Fireworks at night
What a beautiful sight,
Up in the sky,
Falling down from up high,
Is that a portal to a world up high,
Or a group of stars falling down from the sky?
The shapes are cool,
The noises are loud,
The sparkles come showering onto the ground,
See what *fireworks* can do,
Bring the family together,
A joyous occasion as such should last
forever . . .

Karan Sihra (8)
Reddiford School

Seasons

Autumn, winter, summer and spring
These are the seasons we all live in.
Sparkly snow at the top of the mountain,
Flowing water blooming up like a fountain.
Thunder and lightning,
It's really frightening.
Showery rain,
Going down the drain.
In spring flowers pop out,
'It's springtime,' I shout.
Sunny days, palm trees grow coconuts,
Elephants are sweating and want peanuts,
Hot sunny days I have a lot of cool ice lollies,
I go outside and play with my little dollies.
Summer, I go to the seaside,
And lie with some shells near my side.
Sunshine everywhere,
Rain nowhere,
So many seasons,
So many reasons.

Sonal D Patel (8)
Reddiford School

A Place

It was a place which
I would call my home,
a place full of tone,
with colours as bright
as a candy cone.

I eat my ice cream
in this place so sweet
where I have my dreams,
wistful, cosy, secret thoughts.

Leaves a-falling,
birds a-calling,
flowers blooming,
scents and smells.
Each book unfolds a different story,
in this place I would call my home.

Fresh are the winds
that have passed by me.
Wet are the showers that have touched my face.
Cold are the nights that have engulfed me.
Long are the hot sunny days.
Special are the moments in
my private wondrous *place*.

Elisha Patel (9)
Reddiford School

Fireworks

Fireworks shoot up like bullets and they sink
Down like fiery rain
Fireworks make pictures
Like Grandad and Grandma
And they wave right back at you
Before they disappear.

Then the fun starts
The fireworks jump high into the
Air and then *bang! bang! bang!*
They drop down in all sorts of different
Colours like the rainbow.

Now it's time to go away
The fun has come to an end
But don't worry it will
Come next year again.

Sharukh Zuberi (8)
Reddiford School

First Day Back

First day back at school
Dressed in clean and neat uniform
Shiny black shoes on tiny feet.

School hall smells of polish
Children lined up for assembly
Faces full of hope.

Children settle down in classroom
Desks all clean and shiny
Children start new books.

The first bell rings
And children all rush out
For their first play
In the same old playground.

First day back at school.

Nikita Radia (8)
Reddiford School

Fireworks

They glitter in the sky,
That makes it look so bright
There comes a shower of rain,
Of sapphire, purple and pink.

They sparkle in my eye like a
Twinkle in the sky,
They illuminate so bright, like
The starry night.

Like fountains that shimmer
And scream,
Each wonderfulness unfolds
And rockets began to zoom.
Catherine wheels whizzed and
Sizzed.

Air bombs go shooting up
And explode
Bangers go bang and
Make a noise,
Twisters go round and
Round making swirl
Patterns of beautiful
Colours.

Devika Chudasama (9)
Reddiford School

The Creepy-Crawly

There's a spider in my sock.
There's a spider in my coat.
Oh why, oh why doesn't it leave me?

It followed me to school.
It followed me back home.
Oh when, oh when will it go?

It crawled into my sister's bed
And gave her a great big fright.
Mum and Dad rushed in,
'What's the matter?' they exclaimed.
'There's a spider in my bed,'
my sister cried,
'It's on my head!'

Mum caught it,
Dad squashed it.
Splat!
I was alone at last.

The next day,
I had no spider in my sock.
I had no spider in my coat.
Oh what a relief.
Oh phew!

Jonathan Collier (8)
Reddiford School

When I Saw A Dragon

The devouring dragon roared at the sight of me.
His mean red eyes glimmered in the light like two fiery meteorites.
He had two devil-like horns on each side of his monstrous head.
His back was shaped like a stegosaurus.
His beady eyes stared at me as though I were his worst enemy.
He breathed out two enormous fireballs that lingered in the air.
I froze, this was my worst nightmare.
And just as the dragon was lifting up one of his gigantic, scaly legs
as though to charge at me,
I ran away!

Matthew Rodin (8)
Reddiford School

Spiders

They eat the flies
and go up the drains
then in the bath and out

Some are fat and
some are thin
some are hairy
some are not

Some are white
some are black
even poisonous
or ugly maybe not

They live on webs
made out of silk
but do not touch
the web or *snap!*
they bite.

Shivan P Lakhani (8)
Reddiford School

The Poisonous Snake

The poisonous snake was slithering like a sausage,
The deadly snake speaks a different language,

With a quiver the mortal snake bites a human,
Who is the human? Is it you or me? Guess,

The fatal snake calls all his friends,
Because he wants them to eat with him,

The toxic snakes had a tasty dinner,
The dinner was you!

Well, they slept right after their supper,
But just be careful because there might be one just next to *you!*

Gabriel Rajan (9)
Reddiford School

Seasons

Spring
The first time of the year
The birds spread their wings
With no fear

Summer
Starting to get hot
The children will not suffer
Play with the robots

Autumn
The leaves fall down
Starts to get cold
When the trees are bold

Winter
It's Christmas!
It's really cold
It doesn't snow in December.

Kaveer Patel (8)
Reddiford School

The Sun

Slowly rising above the horizon,
Illuminating the dark.
A blaze of crimson and amber,
Accompanied by the sweet song of the lark.

Patiently warming our world,
Perseveringly giving warmth and light.
A huge sphere of burning gas,
Making our earth beautiful and bright.

Our sun is a radiant glow,
Giving with a motherly air.
Smiling down at her children,
Bursting with love and care.

Slowly sinking beneath the horizon,
In a radiance of gold and vermilion.
Vanishing below as the sky darkens,
As the day comes to its termination.

Tejuswi Patel (11)
Reddiford School

The Eerie Castle

The eerie castle coloured in dark grey,
Too much for even a sovereign to pay.
Just then I saw a glint of green,
Nothing could get through it not even a skean.
A green goblin leaping out,
It had a very strange snout,
It leapt out faster than a jack-in-the-box,
He had the same pointed face as a fox,
Was it a dream?
Because if it was, it was extreme.

William Kanagaratnam (8)
Reddiford School

Rainbow

Rainbow, rainbow
So bright in the sky
I love you, I love you
Please don't say goodbye

All the colours
Red, orange, yellow, green, blue, indigo and violet
Make me want to play outside with you

Please stay, please stay
Don't go away
I don't know when I'll see you again

Rainbow, rainbow
So bright and colourful in the sky
You are like a colourful bridge
Swaying ridge to ridge
And staying by my side

Don't go, don't go
My colourful friend
You are a beautiful rainbow
Shaped end to end.

Kushal N Patel (9)
Reddiford School

The Snowman

A bumpy carrot nose,
a crooked smile made of small lumps of coal.
Shiny black eyes that look through you.
A face as white as a ghost, only a lot friendlier.
Smoking grandfather's pipe -
wearing a tweed hat and a coat
two sizes too big -
which is constantly tugged at by a small dog.

But he doesn't care and he doesn't twitch,
this strange man of snow.

Instead he will be left to stand there
all alone - when the children have stopped playing,
the dogs have stopped barking and the babies crying
and their mothers have ceased their non-stop chatter.

For when they return,
he will be gone and only the carrot,
lumps of coal, pipe and coat remain . . .

Kishan Ragunathan (l0)
Reddiford School

Mummy, What Was An Otter?

Each streamlined body
streaking through the water,
each pair of eyes fixed on finding food,
each hand grabbing prey,
each mouth eating a meal,
unchanged since time began.

Each nose sensing food,
each leg kicking through the water,
each ear listening for prey,
each tail keeping them streamlined,
unchanged since time began.

Freddie MacCormack (10)
St Stephen's CE Junior School, Twickenham

Mummy, What Was A Shark?

Each nose was tuned to the smell of blood,
Each jaw was filled with power;
Each eye scanning the sea
Unchanged since time began.

Each head raised and ready
As they prey throughout each day
And the timeless paths of the ocean
Echoed with deadly calls.

Now the ocean is silent,
The smell of blood is gone,
What was once a battlefield
Is now an empty ground.
Now only scavengers
Rule the sea
And the kings of the ocean
Are left to die.

Before we are silenced
Hear our song
Before we are silenced
Hear our cry.

Oscar Allan (9)
St Stephen's CE Junior School, Twickenham

Mummy, What Was A Dolphin?

Each fin looked to the sea,
Each nose jumped to the sky,
Each sleek body speeding through the waves,
Unchanged since time began.

Each fin was touched in greeting,
As they swam through each new dawn
And the timeless paths of the sea
Echoed with dolphin trails.

Now the seas are dark,
The trails are gone.
What was once an ocean,
Has turned into nothing.
Now only plankton drift
Through the empty sea.
The queens of the ocean
Are left to die.

Before we are silenced
Hear our song.
Before we are silenced.
Hear our cry.

Edward McDonald (10)
St Stephen's CE Junior School, Twickenham

Mummy, What Was A Panda?

Each paw was turned to bamboo
each stomach was facing the sun
each forehead was drowned in the blazing sun
unchanged since time began . . .

Each mouth was holding bamboo
as they slept from each new dusk
and woke from each new dawn . . .

Now the forests are lonely
now they lie in darkness
waiting to be found
changed since time ended . . .

Hear our prayer to save us,
hear our song, let us live in peace . . .

Phoebe Evans (10)
St Stephen's CE Junior School, Twickenham

A Waste Of Time

Telling the cameras not to flash.
Telling the dogs not to wag.
Telling potatoes not to mash.
Telling parents not to nag.
Telling Mary not to be hairy.
Telling trees not to have leaves.
Telling monsters not to be scary.
Telling honey trees not to have bees.
Telling wells not to have deep holes.
Telling hair not to have fleas.
Telling lawns not to have moles.
Telling weasels not to wheeze.
Telling football players not to score goals.
Telling people not to have knees.

Ben Bradshaw (8)
St Stephen's CE Junior School, Twickenham

Mummy, What Was A Polar Bear?

Each ear was frosted by the chilly wind of the Atlantic,
Each foot was set upon the ice,
Each coat of fur was used against the cold,
Unchanged since time began.

Each they wore on,
As they swayed from each new dawn,
And the timeless paths of the Arctic
Echoed with the moaning.

Now the seas are plain,
The tracks have disappeared,
What was once the freezing island,
Has turned to water.
Now only polluting ships,
Pollute what's left over,
Once the rings of the ice,
Are left to die.

Before we are silenced,
Hear our song,
Before we are silenced,
Hear our cry.

Eddy Reichwald (9)
St Stephen's CE Junior School, Twickenham

The Key Of The Ancient City

This is the key of the ancient city
In that ancient city there is a town
In that town there is a street
In that street there is a house
In that house there is a staircase
Up that staircase there is a door
Through that door there is a bedroom
In that bedroom there is a bed
On that bed there was a cat
In that cat there was a mouse
In that mouse there was *cheese!*

In that cheese there is a mouse
In that mouse there is a cat
In that cat there is a bed
In that bed there is a bedroom
In that bedroom there is a staircase
In that staircase there is a house
In that house there is a street
In that street there is a town
In that town there is an ancient city.

Olivia Day (9)
St Stephen's CE Junior School, Twickenham

Mummy, What Was A Shark?

Each fin pointing in all directions,
Each eye looking at its prey,
Every gill taking in the salty water of the ocean,
Unchanged since the sea was made.

Each razor-sharp tooth always ready to bite
As it swam along,
And time went by;
Each bone stiff, ready for a fight.

Now the sea is safe,
No more blood is spilt,
Deadly creatures are no more;
And no more do the fish fear,
The seas are now much nicer.

Before we were gone,
Here we were sorry,
Before we were gone,
We did nothing wrong.

Michael Howe (9)
St Stephen's CE Junior School, Twickenham

Mighty Jungle

This is the mighty jungle
In that jungle there is a path
Down that path there is a door
In that door there is a hall
Down that hall there is some light
In that light there is a waterfall
Through that waterfall there is a cave
Down that cave there is an opening
Through that opening there is a tree.

Fionn McKnight (10)
St Stephen's CE Junior School, Twickenham

The Hare And The Tortoise

A hare showed off to a tortoise one day,
'You're a great deal slower than me!'
The tortoise was tired of the boasting hare
And he said, 'I disagree.'

The hare and the tortoise went off
To sort their race plans,
'That tortoise doesn't stand a chance.'
And the tortoise said, 'That hare ain't got no fans.'

The next day the hare was behind the line
Ready to start the race.
Then the tortoise came up behind the line
And the hare said, 'Look at you and your slow pace.'

They started the race
And the hare went into the lead.
The hare went on boasting all the way saying,
'That tortoise is slower than a growing seed.'

The hare zoomed round the track at incredible speed
While the tortoise kept saying his catchphrase
'Slow and steady wins the race.'
The hare just kept on speeding thinking *that tortoise must be in a daze.*

The hare felt tired and laid down for a nap
Whilst thinking *I'll win the bet,*
The tortoise came up to the dozing hare and thought
He looks so peaceful dozing, I'll just let . . .

Finally the hare woke up from his dreams
About winning the race for sure
He got up and stretched
While the tortoise thought *the hare is so poor.*

The hare spotted the tortoise as he was passing the line
And when he passed the line the crowd gave out a roar
And the hare wanted to scream
But he had frozen right to his core.

Nathan King (9)
St Stephen's CE Junior School, Twickenham

Mummy, What Was A Coloured Parrot?

Each ear was turned to the trees,
Each wing stretched out to the sun
Each colour doomed against the sky
Unchanged since time began.

Each head was raised in greeting
As it searched for prey on the branches
And the timeless winds in the trees
Echoed with the whistling song.

Now the skies are dark
The slow, shrill song has gone
What was once a forest
Has turned to stone
And the queens of the forest
Are left to die.

Before we are silenced
Hear our song
Before we are silenced
Hear our cry.

Louise Taylor (9)
St Stephen's CE Junior School, Twickenham

Mummy, What Was A White Tiger?

Each eye focused on its prey
Each claw as sharp as a butcher's knife
Each leg ready to pounce
Unchanged since time began.

Each roar made it ungreeting
As they feed their cubs on bloodied meat
And the timeless parts of South Africa
Echoed with the calling of the roars.

Now the skies are saddened
The meat has gone.
What was once a pride
Is now air.
Now only bugs crawl across the land
As they fill the caves
And the kings of the forest are fading,
No longer seen again.

Thomas Alington (10)
St Stephen's CE Junior School, Twickenham

Night

As shadows creep across my wall,
The ghouls are partying in my hall.
I think there are monsters under my bed,
Or maybe I'm dreaming it in my head.
Do I hear a distant scream?
Or is it just a scary dream?
I pull my duvet way up high,
And lie there hoping they'll pass me by.
A violent screeching of an owl,
A fearsome predator on the prowl.
My face distorts as I yawn,
I'm looking forward to the breaking dawn.

Max Ambler (9)
St Stephen's CE Junior School, Twickenham

Mummy, What Was A Tiger?

A creature sprinting through the grass
Killing as he went
He only stopped to feed his cubs
And his life was only for rent.

He lay and waited for hours and hours
Looking for his prey
But little did the tiger know
The rest of his life was in days.

Now the forests have been demolished
The grass is grey and plain
And the Bengal and Siberian tiger
Are no longer here to reign.

Before we are silenced
Hear our roar
Before we are silenced
Hear our cry.

Christy Born (10)
St Stephen's CE Junior School, Twickenham

This Is Just To Say

I have eaten
your sugar strawberries
in the fridge
even though you were saving them.
Forgive me but I have to say
you always tell me
that people are wasting food in this house
but they were so sweet and juicy.

Alice Hollyer (10)
St Stephen's CE Junior School, Twickenham

Mummy, What Was A Panda?

Each ear was tuned to the forest
Each nose was sniffing the air
Its gentle body pads through the undergrowth
Unchanged since time began.

Each paw was carefully placed on the ground
Each eye was black and round
Each head was raised to the treetops
And the overgrown paths of the forest became used again.

Now the sky is grey
All the tracks have gone
What was once a light place
Has been plunged into darkness
Now only man parades in the forest
And the lives of the pandas are gone forever.

Before we are silenced
Hear our cry
Before we are silenced
Hear our song.

Anna Smethurst (10)
St Stephen's CE Junior School, Twickenham

Elegy

Mummy, what was a panda?

Each ear was tuned to the forest birds,
Each paw reached up to the rays of the sun,
Each head bowed down to the forest
Unchanged since time began.

It's head was focused on a stick of bamboo chewing away,
As the gentle soft animal crawls away.

Now the paths of the animals so quiet and soft have gone;
What was once a bed and home for a panda has gone;
Now the wonderful black and white animals have gone.

Before we are silenced, hear our song;
Before we are silenced, hear our cry.

Laura Goldup (9)
St Stephen's CE Junior School, Twickenham

Elegy

Mummy, what was a cheetah?

Each eye turned upon its prey
Each face was turned against the sun
Each body doomed against man
Unchanged since the world began

Its vast as it sprints through the savannah
Its skin as tough as a rug from the floor
And timeless speed was gone
Its fur to lay down its life
Its skin used as a warm coat

Before we are silenced
Hear our roar
Before we are silenced
Hear our cry.

Eloise Cottey (9)
St Stephen's CE Junior School, Twickenham

Elegy

Mummy, what was a tiger?

Each ear was tuned to the jungle
Each tail was turned up to the sun
Its long body strides through the undergrowth
Unchanged since time began.

Each claw carefully dipped into the water
Each head was raised to the trees
Each eye was small, black and beady
The roaring of the lions
And the hissing of the snakes had disappeared.

Now the skies are dull
The long swishing of the grass has gone
What was a jungle
Has turned into silence
Now only darkness
The jungle is at night
No footsteps in the jungle
And no life.

Sophie Collin (9)
St Stephen's CE Junior School, Twickenham

Mummy, What Was A Rhino?

Each horn was poised to the baking hot sun,
Each ear was startled by the helicopter behind him,
Each foot stampeded through the desert horizon,
Unchanged since time began.

Each tooth chewed on a thick blade of grass
Nothing left to eat
Each hoof was turned as an enemy came by
Not to greet.

Now the skies are grey
Buildings tower over
What was once a desert
Has turned to rotting stone
No trees to look over
Man has taken the throne.

Before we are silenced
Hear our song
Before we are silenced
Hear our cry.

Jack Gregory (10)
St Stephen's CE Junior School, Twickenham

Elegy

Mummy, what was a panda?

Each ear was tuned to the jungle
Each paw reaching out for a bamboo shoot
Each spot on his body stood out
Of the green leaves in the jungle
Unchanged since time began.

Each head raised in greeting
As they watched birds gliding in the sky
And the timeless path of the jungle
Echoed the rustling of the leaves
Now the skies are dark
The paths have gone
What was once a jungle
Has turned to stone
Now only vultures shadow the skies.

And the black and white pandas
Of the jungle are left to die.

Before we are silenced
Hear our song
Before we are silenced
Hear our cry.

Mollie Borges (9)
St Stephen's CE Junior School, Twickenham

My Sweet Drawer

I know it sounds stupid
To have a sweet drawer
But I can't stop collecting
I just keep getting more and more

At the dead of night
I get out of bed
Open the drawer like it's being fed
Put one in my mouth
And climb back into bed

But you see one day
I went on a holiday to play
And all the sweets went sour
In just about an hour

The gum went rock hard
When I got my birthday card
When I came home on Tuesday
Actually a Tuesday in May
I went up to my sweet drawer
But my sweet drawer was no more

In the end
I gave it a mend
And in June
I said, 'I hope I get more soon.'

Eve Carpenter (10)
St Stephen's CE Junior School, Twickenham

A Zoom Poem

This is the key to England
In England is a city
In that city is a small town
And near that town is a forest
In the forest is a tent
Past the tent is a fire
Around the fire is Robin Hood
And his merry men

The merry men with Robin Hood
Sat around the glowing fire
Past the dark tent
Was the creepy forest
In a small town
Was a city
This is the key to England.

Matthew Morris (9)
St Stephen's CE Junior School, Twickenham

Once Upon A Time

Once upon a time,
In a land that only rhymed,

In which everyone could fly,
No one would cry, no one would die.

This land was full of peace,
And no one would cease,
To ask for a friend,
As friendship never ends.

This peace-giving nation,
Is called my imagination.

If I could think of a world,
After this tale has been told,
I can't.

Maeve Gumbley (10)
St Stephen's CE Junior School, Twickenham

Mummy, What Was A Polar Bear?

Each ear was tuned to the ice,
Each paw facing up to the sun,
Each nose faced up to the sky,
Unchanged since time began.

Each head was raised in greeting,
As they shook from side to side,
And the paths in the slippery ice,
Echoed with the quiet sound of their footprints.

Now, the north is getting colder,
And the footprints have gone,
What was once a home to lots of creatures,
Has become lonely and dark,
Now only humans are there,
And build houses in their homeland,
And the queens of the north pole,
Are left to die.

Before we are silenced, hear our song,
Before we are silenced, hear our cry.

Scarlett Rose Young (9)
St Stephen's CE Junior School, Twickenham

The Box

In a scary, scary city
There is a scary, scary street
In the scary, scary street
There is a scary, scary hill
Over the scary, scary hill
There is a scary, scary house
Inside the scary, scary house
There is a scary, scary room
In the scary, scary room
There is a scary, scary box
To open the scary, scary box
You need a scary, scary key
Inside the scary, scary box
There is . . .
A scary, scary house
Which was over a scary, scary hill
Which was in a scary, scary street
And was in a scary, scary city.

Selena Bowdidge (10)
St Stephen's CE Junior School, Twickenham

Millie

I have a friend called Millie
who really looks quite silly!
She's got very frizzy hair
like a shaggy bear,
she's got eyes like the top of milk bottles
like glittery, shiny balls.
She's got a big red nose,
like a huge garden rose.
She's got a very big tummy
like her mummy.
Yes Millie is a sight to see,
but she's as kind as can be.

Faye Driver (8)
St Stephen's CE Junior School, Twickenham

The Storm

The storm roared angrily, ripping leaves off trees,
Tearing plants off the ground like a wolf does its prey.
She swirled round the houses, rattling drainpipes and snatching slates off roofs,
Screaming at the windows and howling through the cracks,
Ripping gates and destroying gardens.
She violently grabbed a tree out of the windswept mud, hurling herself at its battered trunk.
She moved onto the terrified people, wrenching at their umbrellas and seizing their hats in her fiery fists.
She stopped and looked around her.

What she saw was this -

Gates hanging off hinges,
Gardens now a mere swamp of mud,
Trees scattered on the roads,
Lamp posts buried in the roofs of houses,
Mini lakes of muddy water,
People hiding in blown over bus shelters.

My work here is done, she thought
And drifted off leaving it all for the sun to deal with.

Abi Muir (11)
St Stephen's CE Junior School, Twickenham

The Desert

Because of the unrelenting sun,
You have wasted all your supply,
Now you are lamenting,
Because you know that you are going to die.

All your comrades have fallen,
Under the immense heat,
And you are on your own,
Trudging with weary feet.

As you venture on bravely,
The desert creatures scuttle by,
You no longer have any hope,
Because you know that you are going to die.

The skin on your feet,
Is torn to shreds,
As the fleshy remains,
Feel like balls of lead.

By the evening,
As the sun moves by
Your corpse lies on the ground,
But at least you knew that you were going to die.

William Atkins (10)
St Stephen's CE Junior School, Twickenham

My True Dream

There once was a man of Peru,
Who dreamed he was eating his shoe,
He awoke in the night,
With a terrible fright,
Found out it was perfectly true!

Daisy White (11)
St Stephen's CE Junior School, Twickenham

The Magic Box
(Based on 'Magic Box' by Kit Wright)

I will put in my box . . .

The second sunset on a silent night
The sails of boats flapping in the wind
The first sight of a cocooned butterfly

I will put in my box . . .

The claws from a long extinct vicious reptile
A thirteenth hour from a long lost day
And a never-ending story written by the One

I will put in my box . . .

A forgotten island from a distant sea
The blooming flower coming with the rising of the sun
The last wave crashing on a golden beach

My box is fashioned from fire, lightning and lead
With dew on the lid and hope in the nooks and crannies
And its hinges are made from the swords of elves

I shall sail in my box . . .

The wind filling my canvas sails
And I will land in a sunlit cove
The colour of the skins of seals.

Edward Brent (11)
St Stephen's CE Junior School, Twickenham

The Writer Of This Poem
(Based on 'The Writer Of This Poem' by Roger McGough)

The writer of this poem is
As cunning as a cat,
As cool as a cucumber,
Round as a hat.

As forgetful as a fish,
As thick as an elephant,
He likes a Chinese dish,
Always triumphant.

As strong as a lion,
As fast as Dwain Chambers,
His real name is Ryan,
He doesn't like strangers.

He is as ugly as a pig,
As fat as a whale,
He is very big,
Who tells bad tales.

Ryan Alexander, Ben Montgomery & Louis Thrumble (8)
St Stephen's CE Junior School, Twickenham

A Waste Of Time

Telling pigs not to be fat,
Telling cats not to lie on the mat.
Telling rain not to fall,
Telling rugby players not to throw the ball.
Telling smells not to stink,
Telling girls not to like pink.
Telling cars not to drive by,
Telling Grandpa not to die.

Michael Karpathios (9)
St Stephen's CE Junior School, Twickenham

A Waste Of Time

Telling skunks not to stink.
Telling birds not to cry.
Telling pigs to stop being pink.
Telling Grandad not to die.
Telling the toilet not to flush.
Telling rulers not to snap.
Telling Mum not to blush.
Telling the phone not to ring.
Telling gloom not to strike.
Telling sparrows not to sing.
Telling thorns not to prick.
Telling plants not to grow.
Telling food not to decay.
Telling Dad not to sew.
Telling my brother not to play.

Max Tomlinson (8)
St Stephen's CE Junior School, Twickenham

Winter Poem

Outside is as cold as an icicle
Inside the house at Christmas time
Is as warm as the sun
The children are as joyful as Christmas.

A tree's branches at Christmas time
Are as bald as a summer sheep
Outside the children's cheeks are as red as a ruby
The robin's chest is as red as fire.

Eleanor Brent (8)
St Stephen's CE Junior School, Twickenham

The Writer Of This Poem
(Based on 'The Writer Of This Poem' by Roger McGough)

The writer of this poem is
Smaller than a house,
As strong as an elephant,
As steady as a silent mouse.

As light as a feather,
As busy as a bee,
As wild as the weather,
As green as a tree.

As sharp as a knife,
As wise as an owl,
As long as his life,
As flat as a towel.

The writer of this poem
Never ceases to amaze,
He's one in a million billion,
(Or so the poem says).

Lucy Stansbury (9)
St Stephen's CE Junior School, Twickenham

Things I Have Been Doing Lately . . .

Things I have been doing lately . . .
I've been keeping a secret.
I've been pretending to go mad.
I've been jumping up and down.
I've been trying new drinks like brandy.
I've been seeing how long I can hold my breath.
I've been making codes and trying them out.
I've been seeing how much I can read.
I've been spying on my brother.

Rory Atkins (9)
St Stephen's CE Junior School, Twickenham

The Writer Of This Poem
(Based on 'The Writer Of This Poem' by Roger McGough)

The writer of this poem is
as big as a house
as wise as a barn owl
as wriggly as a woodlouse

as fast as a cheetah
as fierce as a dinosaur
as smelly as a pile of rubbish
as scary as a tiger's roar

as light as a hummingbird
as busy as a bee
as cool as a cucumber
as annoying as a flea.

The writer of this poem
never ceases to amaze
he's one in a million billion
(or so the poem says!)

Georgia Beatty (9)
St Stephen's CE Junior School, Twickenham

Winter Poem

It is winter and it is as cold as an icicle.
Everyone has a hat, scarf and gloves.
The frost on my car is as hard as a rock.
The first bit of snow and my heart is full of joy.
'All the kids are as happy as hippies,' my mum says.
The fire is as hot as a volcano.
The ice is as slippery as an ice rink.
We are making a snowman.

Annaliese Dillon (9)
St Stephen's CE Junior School, Twickenham

The Writer Of This Poem
(Based on 'The Writer Of This Poem' by Roger McGough)

The writer of this poem is
As small as a fly
As steady as a stone wall
As good as gold.

As fierce as a tiger
As powerful as a god
As false as a lie
As soft as a rabbit.

As old as an elephant
As busy as a bee
As patient as a pikestaff
As mad as a March hare.

The writer of this poem
Never ceases to amaze
She's one in a million billion
(Or so the poem says!)

Martha Owen (8)
St Stephen's CE Junior School, Twickenham

Winter Poem

The snow is as white as a polar bear
Children's cheeks are as red as a rose
The town is as bare as a mummy's tomb
And the robins are as small as my toes.

The icicles are as hard as a rock
The sky is as scary as ghosts
The houses are as warm as the sun
And the stars are as bright as lamp posts.

Joseph Jackson (8)
St Stephen's CE Junior School, Twickenham

The Writer Of This Poem

The writer of this poem is
As clever as a computer
As small as a mouse
As fast as a cheetah

As fierce as a lion
As happy as a clown
As strong as a boxer
As cold as ice

As mean as a burglar
As cruel as a whip
As loud as a scream
As rude as a punk

The writer of this poem
Never ceases to amaze
He's one in a million billion
(Or so the poem says).

Joseph Whittall (8)
St Stephen's CE Junior School, Twickenham

Winter Poem

As cold as ice.
The trees are as bare as a cloud,
The children as happy as hippos.
The snow is as clean as a newly bought shirt,
And frost is as sharp as a knife.
The houses are as warm as the sun,
As cheerful as a reindeer,
As small as an ice flake,
As strong as a wrestler,
But as daft as a brush.

James McLennan (9)
St Stephen's CE Junior School, Twickenham

The Boy With A Bad Ending

Over a wooden bridge
Through a pond
Past a log
By a signpost
Over a steep hill
Into a garden
Through a shed
Into an abandoned cottage
Up some stairs
Into a room
Under a bed
Down a secret passage
Where a killer waits
In its lair
Look at it, it's a bear
Run away! Run away!
I can never go there
Again.

Oscar Addis (9)
St Stephen's CE Junior School, Twickenham

Winter Poem

Children are as happy as a hippo at Christmas
Mums and dads are as busy as a bee in winter
In England the rain is as wet as the ocean
In winter the houses are as white as snow
The houses are as hot as fire
The badgers sleep as silent as a graveyard.

Sam Norman (9)
St Stephen's CE Junior School, Twickenham

Mummy, What Was A Tiger?

Each ear was tuned to the forest
Each tail stretched out to the sun
Its swift body chased through the trees
Unchanged since time began.

Each paw was raised in greeting
As they prowled from each sunset
And the timeless paths of the forest
Echoed a purring song.

Now there are no more trees for a forest
The skies are dark and cold
What was once a joyful, happy place
Has turned so quiet and deserted
No longer can the prince of the forest be seen
The cold was too much to take.

Before we were silenced
Hear our song
Before we were silenced
Hear our cry.

Georgia Skinner (10)
St Stephen's CE Junior School, Twickenham

Liverpool

My name is Satvinder
My favourite football team is Liverpool
My favourite players are Owen and Kewell
They can all score goals
I would go to Anfield
I would like to see the stadium
They won the Worthington Cup
In the Millennium Stadium
Against Manchester United.

Satvinder Khangoora (9)
The Cedars Primary School

The Cedars School

The Cedars School is a good place to be
You can go on trips and it is wicked
You can play football with your friends
We have a good playground
Where you can play lots of games
There is a tuck shop
Where you can get lots of sweets
They do you lots of toast and I like it too
It is a good place to be.

George Baker (9)
The Cedars Primary School

My Mum

My mum is nice
She cares for me
She lets me in her nice car
I love my mum
She lets me watch TV
She plays battleships with me
She lets me play my PS2
She lets me buy toy cars.

Jordan Anthony (10)
The Cedars Primary School

Emotions

Mrs Kelly makes me happy
My mum makes me surprised
Some people make me sad
My dad makes me happy
Some people hurt me.

Nadia Medjkoun (8)
The Cedars Primary School

War

People are dying everywhere
Sadness is all around
Guns are firing In the air
Bombs fall down and hit the ground
Violence is everywhere
Planes are up in the air
All hope is gone
The battlefield is like a graveyard
With many people dead
All the soldiers have been put to rest.

Philip Hook (10)
The Cedars Primary School

My Family

Me, myself, my mum, my dad
All around I have love and joy to share
I have pure love for my family
When I look into their eyes
It's like they spread their love through the air
I love my family ever so much
I will never leave them in my whole entire life.

Ryan Wilkinson (10)
The Cedars Primary School

Emotions

Surprised is working harder
Sad is when people hurt me
Happy is when Aunty Carla and Kiana take me out
Angry is when I lose my target
Worried is when people are racist
Scared is when I am in the dark.

Kamilha Imran (8)
The Cedars Primary School

Happy

Happy is when my brother gets on with me
And doesn't beat me up
Happy is when my mum does not shout at me
Happy is when my dad does not use his angry voice at me,
My brother and my mum
Happy is when my mum and dad do not have a row
Happy is when I am good and I get sweets
Happy is when I get an award
And I am good most of the time.

Ryan Warner (8)
The Cedars Primary School

Bonfire

Bonfire with lots of sticks
Fireworks going off
Hearing the wind howling in the air
Seeing Guy Fawkes burning in the bonfire
People huddling up around the fire singing songs
As it gets cold people putting on coats
Then the bonfire night comes to an end
People go inside
Then the lights go out.

Marcus Row (9)
The Cedars Primary School

Emotions

Angry is when people wind me up
Hurt is when bad people hit - ouch!
Worried is when I don't have play and I want it
Happy is being kind to people
Scared is when I go in the dark.

Luis Velaquez (7)
The Cedars Primary School

Prison

It's big and the outside is ugly
Desolate and all alone
I think the people in it
Think it's not like home
I would be scared if I had to go there
Just me on my own
Bars outside the windows
Inside the doors of the cell
Inside the cell it's small and cramped
I'm sad, lonely and all alone as well
The floorboards are creaking
Keeping me awake
My sheet is my shield
Against all my bad dreams.

Thomas McKenna (10)
The Cedars Primary School

War

Oh so terrible, dark and grey
Life's blood draining away
Oh so, scared I want to live
The bombs explode and bullets whizz.

Home sweet home, my memory fades
All I hear is people crying
And pleading for life.
Here I am in a corner without a hope
And my soul is sinking.
Do my family know how bad this place is?
Oh they can't, they can't it is too bad.

Now my life is a misery
From the bad and terrible event.

Ciara Spencer (10)
Twickenham Preparatory School

In The Window Display

Looking in at the window display,
Mouth drooling,
Face sweating,
'Can I go inside?' I pray.

But my mother says quick as a flash,
'No, I've got places to be
People to see
Can't go in there right now.'

After school going home,
Passing the sweet shop display.
Stop for a moment,
'I'll go inside,' I say.

Turn to the jars of everything,
Dig my hand in every one.
Pay for the lot,
Pull my bike out its parking slot.
See you tomorrow window display!

Claire Leslie (10)
Twickenham Preparatory School

There Are Ants In My Food

There are ants in my food,
What shall I do?
They are crawling everywhere.

There are ants in my food,
What shall I do?
They are on my bacon roll.

There are ants in my food,
What shall I do?
They are eating all my food.

There are ants in my food,
I know what to do,
Poke them with my fork!

Gordon Parker (10)
Twickenham Preparatory School

Heaven

When Mother Nature brings life to a close,
It may be the end of earthly living,
But the heavenly life is just beginning.
Where silver winged angels and chubby faced cherubs
Start the loving and happy times.

You are woken in the depths of the night,
With a golden, lit stairway before you
And an angel is right by your side
Tugging you to follow her away.

When you reach Heaven you'll be able to see,
The candyfloss flooring and rainbow roomed homes
And to feel the burden be lifted off your shoulders
By floating little cherubs with twinkling smiles on their faces.

The food you eat will never go cold,
Your hearts will never go empty
So do not fear your afterlife,
Just imagine the glorious moments.

Amy-Ciara Turner (11)
Twickenham Preparatory School

My Favourite Thing

My favourite thing comes out in spring,
The weather is warm but often wet,
The flowers are budding but not there yet!

The grass underfoot has grown a lot
And there to see her, coming to me at a trot.
Her name is Bonnie, all shiny and black,
I met her for he first time whilst out on a hack.
With a spring in her step and eager to please,
A flick of my whip and she's into the breeze.
This is my favourite thing, she makes me feel free!
One last ride my Bonnie lass,
Set me free - set me free!

Jasmine Pastakia (10)
Twickenham Preparatory School

I Feel Ill

Lying down in bed, ill,
Tummy turning up, ill,
Tonsils flaming up, ill,
I feel ill!

Not going to school, ill,
Can't get to sleep, ill,
Feeling very weak, ill,
I feel ill!

Finding it hard to eat, ill,
Head feeling thick, ill,
Light piercing eyes, ill,
I feel ill!

Got to take a pill, ill,
Mummy coming up, ill,
Feeling quite good, ill,
I am quite ill!

Tummy not turning up,
Feeling very strong,
Eating very well,
I am not ill!

Imogen Thain (10)
Twickenham Preparatory School

Cleo, My Cat

Her silky black fur soft to touch
Tail waving in the wind
Eyes staring as I walk by
Scary, motionless, staring eyes
Sharp hearing ears prick up for sound
And her tail goes up when another cat is nearby.
Her fat tummy wobbles as she walks, away from another huge meal
She likes to be stroked with warm, firm hands along her back
That's Cleo my cat!

Harriet Page (9)
Twickenham Preparatory School

Flowers

Amongst a garden full of grass
Are hidden flowers that grow so fast.
First they start as seeds
Then some grow to weeds.

      Some of them are beautiful
      And look kind like me.
      Some of them are ugly
      Like some people I see
      Some are full and bushy
      While others smell like Chinese sushi.

There are stripy ones
And spotty ones
And multicoloured other ones.
The sunflower is tall and bright
While the primrose is small and dull.

      They brighten up the place
      And put a smile on everyone's face
      After seeds they begin to sprout
      Then their stems seem to look about.

Did you know when the pollen grows
A bee can smell it with its tiny nose.
Bees collect honey
Which tastes perfect for my tummy!

Hayley Dixon (10)
Twickenham Preparatory School

The Changing Year

January	As we celebrate the New Year Everyone is in good cheer.
February	The special months with the shortened day Brings a lot of frosty haze.
March	As spring comes into the air Baby lambs and flowers are everywhere.
April	A time for joking and playing the fool Especially on the teachers at school.
May	The bank holiday Mondays Turn the normal Mondays into fun days.
June	As all the summer school events come up The winning team receive a cup.
July	We all head off on holiday To our secret hideaway.
August	Everyone is having fun Playing and swimming in the sun.
September	As the days start to get cool Time to think about going back to school.
October	As we turn the clock back The nights get very black.
November	As the autumn leaves fall The Christmas organisations call
December	As everyone receives our presents We all eat turkey, ham and pheasants.

Lloyd Allen (11)
Twickenham Preparatory School

The Seaside

Every year I come to play,
Beside the shore is where I'll stay.
With my swimsuit on
And sunhat,
I surely won't want to leave.
Slap the suncream on I say,
Be careful not to catch some rays!

Whatever to do next
I think I'll have a rest
So I get down on my towel
And lie until I doze in the sun.
There is Mum buying me a bun,
I can't wait to get it in my tum.

Today we are going to the fair
I don't think Mum has much care
The ride I want to go on has a dragon's lair
With white teeth it is not real
Poor Dad it's really not that bad.

I wonder what to do today
I know, let's go and play.
Please Mum can we get a blow up boat
I promise not to say a quote.
So off I go in my inflatable boat
Trying to keep afloat.

The sad time has come
When we will all become
Ourselves again not playing on the beach
But instead the beach is out of reach
For this was all a dream to me
The seaside is a magic place you see.

Sarah Hopkin (10)
Twickenham Preparatory School

The Kallacacoon

With eyes of fire
And a body of flames,
Half lion, half man
It is anything but tame.

When its high-pitched call
Spreads through the land where men dare to tread,
It flexes its claws majestically
And everything in its path falls dead.

When the sound of music drifted into its lair one day
From a weary traveller's flute,
The soothing music calmed the beast
Like the music of strings, lyre and lute.

When the beast awoke the very next day
Out of the cave it came,
It went into the city
Bright, cheerful and tame.

Andrew Home (11)
Twickenham Preparatory School

Winter

A soft white blanket covering everything.
Crunchy snow under your feet,
Flakes falling, falling, always falling,
Soft small balls coming out of the sky,
Silently covering everything and making rough things smooth.

Icicles glistening like crystal daggers,
Sheets of smooth ice hanging everywhere,
Crystal silver daggers threatening to pierce your skin,
Glass stalactites hanging off roofs.

Children having fun ice skating on the frozen ponds,
Boys having snowball fights,
Children having fun in the snow in winter.

Matthew Born (9)
Twickenham Preparatory School

A Stray Bullet

A stray bullet
Could easily take another man's life.
Just imagine if it was your life,
Over in the time it takes to click your fingers.
Everything you know and have known,
Love and have loved -
Gone.
Yet if you were there,
You may even have thought it kind,
A quick end to a long beginning.
A story with nothing but suffering.
Just imagine if it was your family.
A sad telegram sent to them,
The bearer of bad news.
Never able to see your shining face again,
Never able to watch you grow into a young adult,
And then to an old man.
Just imagine if it was your country.
After the war, after they've won.
They'll say thank you to all the people who fought for them,
But they won't remember you.
Very few people will actually remember *you,*
When you're dead.
So just imagine if it was your stray bullet.
Another man's life,
Taken.
Everything he knows and has known,
Loves and has loved -
Gone.

Chloe Gale (10)
Twickenham Preparatory School

The Eye Of The Dragon

Swooping through the night sky
A ship on cloudy seas.
Watch the ghostly figure
Fly between the trees.
Shadows at its clawed fingers
And fire at its beak,
It has a roar that could wake the Kraken,
In its deep, dark keep.

Ragged wings from its shoulders,
And you must see its wicked eyes;
The eyes of a dragon, ruler of the skies.
It is ruler of the sky,
Day and also night.
No one has objected to this,
It's a creature you don't want to fight!

In this harsh world of dragons,
At night you just might see;
Swooping through the night sky,
A ship on cloudy seas.
Watch the ghostly figures
Fly between the trees.

Gwen Owen Jones (9)
Twickenham Preparatory School

Spring

Bunnies are hopping
Lambs are leaping
Jack Frost is thawing
And the snowdrops are peeping

Springtime is here
Let's all give a cheer!

Holly Louise Squires (8)
Twickenham Preparatory School

The Skating Party

When I was ten I took my friends skating
The venue was Hampton Court
People arrived with presents they'd brought
On went the boots with a pull and a tug
Nervously stepping onto the sparkling ice
Eyes twinkling bright.

Vibrant coloured hats glide off to the distance
Twirling round to carols playing
Laughter pushing steamy breath out.

Children falling, voices calling
Cold limbs thawed with soothing hot chocolate
The party ended with girls exhausted
Gloves and trousers dripping wet
Lots of chatter travelling home.

Fleur Kenny
Twickenham Preparatory School

Solitary Child

A whisper of a tree,
The stillness of the night,
Is all this little girl hears.
The swish of the grass,
The whistle of the wind,
As it travels on its way.
The little girl sits where the grass was green
And where the white daisies were,
Where the birds sang
And the butterflies came and went,
But all has gone from this beautiful land,
Gone and passed away,
Except this girl,
Who sits so still,
Watching over her grave.

Zoë Monckton (10)
Twickenham Preparatory School

Animal Nature

Dogs and cats, fish and rats,
Lizards, lions, tigers, bats,

Animals are all unique,
What kind of creature do you seek?

Cats are sleek, they twist and bend,
Dogs are loyal (man's best friend!)

Bats have sonar, fly by echoes,
Lizards are cute (especially geckos).

Fish are shiny, streamline things,
Lions are royal, jungle kings.

Rats have claws and twitching faces,
Tigers hunt in open spaces.

All animals have different ways -
Different habits, different prey!

Charlotte Matten (10)
Twickenham Preparatory School

The City

The city is a large place,
With paper flying,
Like snow in a blizzard,
Bins falling,
Like glitter floating from tins,
Dingy lights,
Like the evening sun,
Dirty streets,
Like coffee-stained clay blocks,
Tall buildings,
Like giants' colossal bodies,
Loud voices,
Like a wandering echo.

Amy Horrell (9)
Twickenham Preparatory School

The Dragon

In a cave beyond your nightmares,
Lives a beast that never sleeps.
The dragon,
The dragon.
His eyes poisonous marbles,
Teeth covered in blood,
Red blood,
Human blood.
Scales glistening silver,
Spikes studded with jewels,
Sapphires, rubies and emeralds,
Jewels of the kings he's slain.
Roars more terrifying than evil,
Send stalactites down to the floor,
Charred nostrils breathing out fire,
Fire,
Hell's fire.
The door to his lair, always open,
No exit, no man ever leaves.
Beware to all the travellers who seek him,
On his putrid breath linger their screams.

Florence Brady (10)
Twickenham Preparatory School

My Rabbit

I love my dear old rabbit
He has a little habit
He always throws his food bowl down
And he dances like a clown
My grandad calls him
Thumper Bumper.

Rupi Thind (8)
Twickenham Preparatory School

Football

Football is a sport which I adore,
Every day I like it more and more.
The position I play is in strike,
Which I must admit I very much like.
Every morning I practise my skill,
Before the school morning drill.
The best footballer in my year,
Will probably end up with a football career.
He plays like Thierry Henry
And he runs rapidly.
The make of his football boots is Umbro,
And it makes him play like a pro.
Friday is the day I most crave,
My shots the goalie cannot save.
I put the ball at the back of the net,
Even better than Tottenham's Gus Poyet.

Taran Hothi (9)
Twickenham Preparatory School

The Lightning

The lightning was loud, so loud,
Its evil colours show,
The scrape of a cat's claw in the sky.
The blue, purple and white
Kept me awake all night
The sound so piercing
As it broke the silence through the town.

The bolt was like a dagger,
Across the moon, it scraped,
The piercing, jagged edges,
Made the light so bright,
All through the night,
The light so bright.

Emily Jordan (9)
Twickenham Preparatory School

A Steam Engine

A big blue steam engine comes down the track,
Into the station it rolled, clackety clack.
With a great big hiss it grinds to a halt,
With screeching and wailing the carriages stop with a jolt.

People open the doors and board the train,
If you stay the noise will drive you insane.
All the people close the doors with a slam,
They all close them with the force of a ram.

With all doors closed it pulls out the station,
Thundering to its next destination,
Picking up speed with a great big puff,
The journey ahead will be very rough.

Storm clouds are gathering along the way,
The sky further ahead is turning grey.
Faster, faster it has to be on time,
It has to be there when the clock strikes nine.

Cameron Sumner (9)
Twickenham Preparatory School

Paradise

Palm trees are close to the sparkling ocean,
There's a blanket of golden sand,
Children make sandcastles in the sandpit,
Adults sit back and enjoy sunbathing,
Teens explore cliff caving.

You definitely need lots of sun lotion,
The water sports have lots of motion,
The children planned
To bury their parents in the sand,
Everyone parties and sings along to the reggae band.
When the sun sets the sky is red
And this day not another word is said.

Isabelle Manning (9)
Twickenham Preparatory School

The Sea

Thick, foamy, lashing waves
Bubbling, salty, blue and green
Sharp sea
Home to other creatures

The seabed
A beach under water for
Oil fish
Hammerhead
Eel
Shark

Rocks with caves
Hidden by seaweed strips
Flowers with fingers
Gently brushing and floating

The wonder of the sea
Our blue planet
Dark, inviting
The deeper you go.

Francesca Harland (10)
Twickenham Preparatory School